Contemporary Indian Political Theory

Contemporary Indian Political Theory
A Critical Analysis

Dhananjay Rai

AAKAR

Contemporary Indian Political Theory: *A Critical Analysis*
Dhananjay Rai

First Published, 2013

ISBN : 978-93-5002-248-1

Published by
AAKAR BOOKS
28 E Pocket IV, Mayur Vihar Phase I, Delhi 110 091
Phone : 011 2279 5505 Telefax : 011 2279 5641
info@aakarbooks.com; www.aakarbooks.com

Printed at
Mudrak, 30 A, Patparganj, Delhi 110 091

Contents

Acknowledgements

Contemporary Indian Political Theory is neither meant to explore *indigenism* in the form of Indian theory nor surveying the literature. Instead, insertion of 'Indian Political Theory' demonstrates important contemporary Indian developments from the vantage point of political theory. In other words, 'Indian Political Theory' denotes the confluence of contemporary Indian developments and political theory which constitutes a particular time and apace. It critically examines the peculiar Indian responses on certain issues which are vital to probe whether only people's participation is a defining moment of construal of Indian democracy or 'participation' and 'relisation of being participants' are also its sine qua non components.

Accordingly, these chapters were written over the years and discussed in numerous formal and informal academic spaces. Parts of the three chapters (*Freedom of Expression and Liberal Dilemma; B.R. Ambedkar, Freedom and Class of Politics* and *Familial Politics, Familiar Political Class and Democracy*) were discussed in *Pragoti*. Some parts of the fourth chapter (*Dalits, Globalisation and Economism*) were presented as *Dalits, Globalisation and the Issue of Democratic Rights* (for *Student Presentation Series* organised by the Centre for Political Studies Students' Series, SSS-II, Jawaharlal Nehru University, September 18, 2009), *Dalits, Social Justice and Unscrambling the Mystifications of Globalisation Defence:*

Excursus in Recent Trends (for *Affirmative Action Policies and Marginalized Sections in India*, a National Seminar organised by the Department of Political Science, University of Allahabad, February 19-20, 2011) and *Philosophy of Globalization and Cul-de-sac Defence: A Curious Case of India's Margins* (for *Philosophy for New Economic Order*, a National Seminar organised by the Department of Philosophy, Panjab University, Chandigarh, March 29-30, 2011). A part of this chapter also appeared in *Think India Quarterly* (volume 13, No. 3, July–September 2010). I express my gratitude to the seminar organisers for their invitation to participate in seminars and to the journal for the publication of it. The earlier version of the fifth chapter (*Foundational Knowledge and De-decentring Tendency*) was presented as *De-Decentring Higher Education and its Ramifications* (for *Politics Education: Higher Education in India - Context & Concerns (Focus on Madhya Pradesh)*, a National Seminar organised by School of Studies in Political Science & Public Administration, Jiwaji University, Gwalior, March 19-21, 2010) and *Knowledge, De-decentring Tendencies and Implications in India* (for *Higher Education in India: Challenges & Prospects*, a National Seminar organised by Kannur University Union, Research Centre and Central Library, Kannur University, December 13-15, 2011). I am thankful to the organisers for their invitation to respective seminars. A version of this chapter was published in *India Researcher* (2011). I am equally grateful to the editor and the resident editor for their valued comments, review and publication. The sixth chapter (*India, Pakistan and Coalescence History of People*) was partially published in *Think India Quarterly* (volume 14, No. 4, October–December 2011) and *Journal of Interdisciplinary Research and Action* (July, 2013). I am thankful to these two journals for the publication of earlier versions of the chapters.

The personal/institutional support received from Prof. R.K. Kale (Vice Chancellor, Central University of Gujarat), Prof. N. Rajaram, Prof. Ajay Dandekar and Prof. E.V.

Ramakishnan was crucial for the completion of this book. Constant encouragement from Prof. R.K. Kale and critical interactions with Prof. N. Rajaram were immensely helpful. My colleagues at CUG remained the backbone towards the completion of this book. Smruti Ranjan Dhal and Mehak Talwar went through the entire draft painstakingly. Both reread chapter 4 (*Dalits, Globalisation and Economism*) and chapter 2 (*B.R. Ambedkar, Freedom and Class of Politics*) respectively. Maitrayee Mukerji (introductory chapter *Prolegomenon* and chapter 5: *Foundational Knowledge and De-decentring Tendency*), Manasi Singh (chapter 1: *Freedom of Expression and Liberal Dilemma* and chapter 6: *India, Pakistan and Coalescence History of People*), Siba Sankar Mohanty (chapter: *Freedom of Expression and Liberal Dilemma* and chapter: *Familial Politics , Familiar Political Class and Democracy*), Beryl Anand (chapter 6: *India, Pakistan and Coalescence History of People*), Priya Ranjan Kumar (introductory chapter *Prolegomenon* and chapter 3: *Familial Politics , Familiar Political Class and Democracy*) have been crucial colleagues and friends who commentated extensively and rigorously on respective chapters. They all forced me to revise the certainty of 'unexplained' and 'given' premises. I am thankful for their frank, honest and rigorous comments on the book.

Rityusha's (JNU) incisive comments and invaluable suggestions on all chapters led to the culmination of the actual form of the present book. Pavel's (JNU) comments (on chapter 1 and 2) were helpful and needed for removing several repetitions. Rityuja's astute comments on language and sentence formation led to the correction of several mistakes. Many thanks to all of them for rendering uncomplaining help and sparing valuable time.

I must acknowledge the years of dialectical learning through the Creative Theory Group (Jawaharlal Nehru University and Delhi University) while not forgetting the immense support of Prof. Manindra Nath Thakur. My gratitude goes to Priti Singh (Delhi University) and Pradipta Kumar Parida for editing the entire draft. I am also thankful to K.K. Saxena of Aakar Books for readily agreeing to publish this book. Barring his unquestioning support, the publication of this book would have remained a distant dream.

Prolegomenon

It depends not on consciousness, but on being; not on thought, but on life; it depends on the individual's empirical development and manifestation of life, which in turn depends on the conditions obtaining in the world. If the circumstances in which the individual lives allow him only the [one]-sided development of one quality at the expense of all the rest, [if] they give him the material and time to develop only that one quality, then this individual achieves only a one-sided, crippled development. No moral preaching avails here. And the manner in which this one, pre-eminently favoured quality develops depends again, on the one hand, on the material available for its development and, on the other hand, on the degree and manner in which the other qualities are suppressed.

—Karl Marx and Frederick Engels, German Ideology (1846) (Marx and Engels, 1976: 262)

In other words, there must be social endosmosis.

—B. R. Ambedkar, Annihilation of Caste (1936) (Ambedkar, 1979: 57)

There is a great need of some one with sufficient courage to tell Indians: 'Beware of parliamentary democracy, it is not the best product as it appears to be...'

—B. R. Ambedkar, Labour and Parliamentary Democracy (1943) [Speech delivered at the concluding session of the All India Trade Union Workers' Study Camp held in Delhi from 8th to 17th September 1943 under the auspices of the Indian Federation of Labour] (Ambedkar, 1991: 107)

Construal of democracy is an inevitable task for the emergence of people's democracy over fragmented democracy. People's democracy or *hoi polloi* democracy entails participation of people in the institutions and their realisation of being participants. Participation and realisation of being participants are both intrinsic aspects of people's democracy. Fragmented democracy prefers participation to realisation of being participants. Liberal democracy is a typical fragmented democracy. The advent of liberal democracy was for participation and not for the realisation of being participants. Participation takes place by way of 'one person, one vote'. 'One person, one vote' has become the universal slogan of liberal democracy. There have been broadly two phases of participation by way of 'one person, one vote' in the realm of liberal democracy. The first phase signalled the decline of a darkened feudal or medieval era. The crumbling of feudal edifice opened up an era of mobility of people and the advent of a different mode of production which had not only generated capital but also enhanced its circulation. The structural demise necessarily generated individual led endeavour. Initially, capitalism opened up the possibility of individual led effort which eventually and necessarily turned out to be the system. Therefore, texts of liberal political theory, written during or after Industrial Revolution, focus on individual right and freedom.

The assumption or theorisation of free individuals takes into account nascent capitalism wherein an individual was really free to mobilise as compared to one in the erstwhile period. However, this mobility ceases with the individual's full integration into the capitalist system. Democracy was the reflection of mobility, i.e. mobility of capital and people. Idea of democracy was to participate in the government by means of 'one person, one vote'. The apothegm and practice of 'one person, one vote' encapsulates two meanings. First, it connotes the recognition of individual as the bearer of right and one's 'own' decision maker/taker. Second, her/his 'own' decision envisages or is based on the apothegm which goes against the inertness of feudal structure. The government can be changed by quirks of majority of individuals. So the idea is based on the idea of mobility. The government is mobile. The origin and functioning of capitalism is also based on dynamism in terms of technological innovation and its changing form from classical capitalism to speculative capitalism. Mobility in democracy and dynamism has one commonality, that is an idea of choice. At the outset, choice appears as an innocent move but it is not. One can choose the government, but choice beyond the government is ruled out. In other words, mobility within the structure is available but mobility beyond is circumscribed. In capitalism also, mobility of being the seller of labour power is possible but the appropriation of surplus value for all is not.

Liberal democratic theorists have been condemned on the following accounts. To begin with, they could not differentiate between individual mobility during nascent days of capitalism and full-fledged capitalist system. In the former case, this mobility was rejuvenating; a promise of arrival of the new being. In the latter case, mobility was reduced for working class and bourgeoisie for labour exploitation and appropriation of surplus value, respectively. Still, liberal democratic theory defines democracy as 'one person, one vote' in the context of nascent capitalism. 'One person, one vote', once a revolutionary epithet, was reduced to the mere process of formation of government sans system transformation. In others words, people are being made or treated as mere *isopsephos*. Eventually, capitalism became the system in which democracy had to work, and individuals' mobility and choice were confined to labour power whereas appropriation of surplus value was confined to a few. Since then, 'one vote, one person' has changed government after government but every government after government has used mobility cum choice *per se* in terms of labour power and surplus appropriations.

The crux of the problem in liberal democratic theory is that there is no recognition of fragmented democracy. 'One person, one vote' ensures government changeability but rules out structural change by reduction of mobility. Here a peculiar condition emerges. Indeed, there is participation but not realisation of being participants. Realisation of being participants can only be possible through people's democracy where participation and being participants both occupy equal spaces. Realisation of being participants is contingent upon equal being. An equal being is different from a similar being. Equal being signals an equal ontological being. The possibility of differentiated treatment and its factors are discarded. A similar being is neither desired nor possible. Marxism emphasises on equal beings, not on similar beings. Any attempt to produce similar beings will eventualise a monotonous and homologous society and a structure as was/is attempted by religious fundamentalists and fascist forces.

The second phase of 'one person, one vote' phenomenon was the extension of this idea to the erstwhile colonial countries by capitalist bloc. Even, democracy has been exported through 'democratic theses', 'colour revolutions' and 'regime change interventions'. It is being told that the successful landmark of democracy is an incessant repetition of electioneering. Participation by 'one person, one vote' *ipso facto* becomes necessary and a sufficient condition. The entire justification is *modus ponens*. In other words, if 'one person, one vote' is equal to democracy, then democracy is functional where and whenever this antecedent takes place. This serves the interest of the system while negating the multiple contradictions.

In this backdrop, Indian democracy or democracy in India needs revaluation which can take place only through crossing '*votering* method', whereby vote is an ultimate truth.

Following this method would suggest that recognition of democracy is not a mere participation by voting. It also includes realisation of being participants. It further suggests that realisation of being participant is achieving the condition of equal beings. And achieving of equal beings is only possible when democracy of *hoi oligoi* is replaced in the true sense by democracy of *hoi polloi*.

Certain trends can be identified, which may invalidate the claim that participation synonymises realisation. There are a plethora of examples whereby reference could be drawn on democracy in India. The limited purpose of *Contemporary Indian Political Theory: A Critical Analysis* is to look into the factors whereby signposts could be drawn regarding inhabiting causes of non-realisation of being participants. The limitation of this book is that it touches only five issues while there are numerous such contemporary issues. These chapters were discussed thoroughly in academic circles and published partially. The revised chapters are being presented here. Five such issues, in six chapters, identified limitedly for this book are freedom, familial politics, globalisation, knowledge and neighbourhood relations.

The first chapter *Freedom of Expression and Liberal Dilemma* discusses the issue of freedom in the context of Salman Rushdie's *non-visit* (January, 2012) to India. This chapter re-evaluates the liberal dilemma over the issue of 'expression'. Rights and expression are intertwined. Expression is a medium whereby violation of rights can be opined. However, rights themselves are not comprehensive. Therefore, expression is also not comprehensive. Only limited expressions are allowed which are linked with limited rights. The liberal dilemma emerges when this limited expression is also violated. This chapter argues that freedom of all which is linked with comprehensive rights can ensure the freedom of few. Freedom of few cannot be a guarantor of freedom of all.

The second chapter *B.R. Ambedkar, Freedom and Class of Politics* also touches upon the complexities of freedom. In India, the presence of a cartoon in the school text book has generated a convoluted debate. Portrayal of B.R. Ambedkar, one of the most important revolutionaries, in a cartoon has invited multiple construals. The Government of India had immediately expunged the cartoon from the school text book and formed a committee to look into other cartoons. The expert committee has recommended the deletion of certain cartoons aiming at politicians and bureaucrats. In the entire debate, B.R. Ambedkar's idea of freedom has been missed. Class of politics, another tool to understand the nature of politics, has also been given a miss. This chapter emphasises on idea of Ambedkar's freedom and class of politics. Class of politics of a political class, which took decision, has to be explained because of the continuous scant attention to B.R. Ambedkar and now because of the intriguing defence of removal of a cartoon in his name.

The third chapter *Familial Politics, Familiar Political Class and Democracy* discusses the two aspects of people's democracy, i.e. participation and realisation of being participants. Familial politics is a particular type of politics wherein succession lines are drawn from the family. Familial politics in turn produces a familiar political class. Familial politics even bypasses the minimum requirement of liberal democracy, i.e. universal participation. A familiar political class again violates the realisation of being participants precisely because it strengthens the theoretical postulation of birth-based privileges. Its corollary is the lessening of struggle against birth-based discrimination. Emergence of a familiar political class also helps them to form coalition for the status quo.

The fourth chapter *Dalits, Globalisation and Economism* at the outset highlights the method of reading globalisation. It circumvents the binary to understand globalisation. It takes recourse to dalit discourse. It rejects preferential treatment to sovereignty over participation and realisation of being participants. It also negates the 'coalescing modernity with globalisation'. Economism emphasises on economic integration, followed by the political and social integration and not otherwise. Globalisation envisages the world as *the global* and does away with the constraints for integration by way of liberalisation and privatisation. For these purposes, globalisation functions through the need principle (availability of resources through negotiations) while rejecting the necessity principle (participation and realisation of being participants whereby participation and resource availability is a non-negotiable issue). The defenders of globalisation argue for the arrival of a new turn by way of globalisation. Nonetheless, they omit four important concerns *vis-à-vis* globalisation, i.e. negation of consequence of globalisation, social reconstruction, the Bhopal Declaration and the much needed comparison between dalit capital and black capital.

The fifth chapter *Foundational Knowledge and De-decentring Tendency* examines the link between foundational knowledge (higher education) and de-decentring tendency (return of centralisation/centralised tendency). Foundation knowledge becomes crucial due to two of its capacities-acquisition and dissemination. Acquisition or acquiring activities entail acquiring investigatory aspects through epochal analysis, contemporary analysis and visionary certitude. Dissemination helps to acquaint people with these analyses. In case of being monopolised by few, it produces de-decentring tendency. The ruling classes adopt different attitude towards functional knowledge (elementary knowledge). Foundational knowledge gets liberated due to arrival of modernity and progressive movements. The struggle in India for foundational knowledge has been done through the claim principle. The neo-liberal project has contravened the claim principle by way of appropriation of the states' foundational knowledge and monopolisation of foundational knowledge. The best possible way to counter the de-decentring tendency is to reinvigorate the claim principle.

The sixth chapter *India, Pakistan and Coalescence History of People* focuses on the construction of India-Pakistan relationship. It highlights the significance of 'coalescence' history that is a history of commons. India-Pakistan relationship has been defined by global forces from the vantage points of 'existence', 'strategic', 'military industry complex', and 'expansion of capitalism'. The ruling classes of both countries have replaced coalescence history with contemporaneity. In other words, 'contemporaneity' history decides the history of both countries. This has produced disastrous consequences. Accordingly, relationship between both countries has been shaped through three realms of 'autonomy', 'contestation' and 'mutual terrain'.

The method, purpose and relevance of the book rest on three edifices. First, an attempt is made to construct people's political theory. Therefore, second, subject matter of the book reflect the prevailing condition of people. Reflection of freedom is also a reflection of prevalent condition. If politics is a method of choice and change, then familial politics is the actual obstruction. Globalisation, as its supporters would argue, enhances opportunities. If it is so, then what is the status of democratic rights? Can opportunities be enhanced in the absence of democratic rights? Knowledge production and control also expose the multi-layered contradiction of globalisation whereby people are being denied access to it. If common history of people becomes liability, then the fault does not lie in commonality but in defining the relation between two countries, who shared common history once upon a time, from contemporaneity. In these ways, this book brings back material resources of political theory from prevalent world which certainly repudiates a priori reasoning and social contract led formulations.

1

Freedom of Expression and Liberal Dilemma

I have no doubt that what has ruined Parliamentary Democracy is idea of freedom of contract. The idea became sanctified and was upheld in the name of liberty.

—B.R. Ambedkar (Ambedkar, 1991: 108)

Freedom of opinion is important for many reasons, especially because it is a necessary condition of all progress, intellectual, moral, political, and social. Where it does not exist, the status quo becomes stereotyped, and all originality, even the most necessary, is discouraged.

—Bertrand Russell (Russell, 1996: 453)

Lexicon of liberal political theory of democracy is replete with virtuous phrases like 'rights' and 'expression'. At the outset, it seems that the riddle between rights and expression is solved conveniently. It is told that rights are a necessary condition for democracy. Its absence can only be known through expression. Rights are legalistic institutional mechanism whereby something is protected and sustained. Expression comes only when rights are violated. Thus everyone can express the genuine absence of rights. The fallacy of this argument is that rights are neither comprehensive nor aptly guaranteed. So, expressions are also neither comprehensive nor aptly guaranteed. Only those expressions which are related with 'limited' rights are allowed. This limited expression is being celebrated virtuously across the board. The problem, the resultant advent of liberal dilemma, arises when even this limited expression is violated in a particular context. The liberal clad and liberal public spheres do not understand why the pristine right of expression is violated. Salman Rushdie's *non-visit* (January, 2012) provides the opportunity to revisit the liberal dilemma.

Signification of Literary Intervention

Since 2006, Jaipur has been witnessing an unorthodox activity in the month of January. January brings each year a conglomeration of writers, academicians and the ilk under the tutelage of Jaipur Literary Festival (JLF). In the state which is marred by feudal remnants and living repercussions of caste atrocities and bestowal of epithets like '*raja*' (king) and '*rani*' (queen), agnatically and consciously, intervention by way of 'literary festival', unknowingly for cause and certainly for luxury due to availability of 'royal' ambience and rosy nature of city is a noticeable watershed regarding liberal intervention. The ability and desire for hybrid conglomeration are fructuous endeavours.

JLF 2012 was in news for all reasons. The invitation by organisers to Salman Rushdie, a writer of many acclaimed books but particularly marked for *Satanic Verses*[1], to participate in this festival to discuss his award winning book *Midnights Children* sparked a quadrupling and flummoxing debate when the vice chancellor of *Darul Uloom* (a Muslim Seminary located at Deoband Uloom, Uttar Pradesh), Maulana Abul Qasim Nomani urged the government to cancel his visa. His visit and alternative options like participation through video conference were annulled. The epithet like right or wrong is avoided by many corners for the time being because multiple construals are still being explored. Numerous nuances that emerged in this festival certainly raise some unpalatable questions. The range of questions could be from 'freedom' to 'right to hurt' to 'right to unhurt'. Unfortunately, debates on many opinionated channels and newspapers in the Indian public sphere were zeroed in on corollary issues and not on the essentiality of problems. The significant question before us today is to address the essentiality of problems which will *ipso facto* solve the corollary issues. Mere focusing on corollary issues will not solve the complex fiasco that unfolded in the JLF.

Making Sense of Corollary and Essentiality

Corollary is an important signature in so far as exhibition of a particular problem is concerned. In the liberal discourse of India, Rushdie's *non-visit* has become a signifier of freedom and rightly so. The organisers, authors and Salman Rushdie have genuine complaint of denial of opportunity of expression. Of course, he is a vantage point in the entire discourse and faced onslaught from numerous corners. Even in primetime debate of news channels for many days, it was all together a Rushdie affair. Liberal channels went on soothingly defending freedom of expression and right to voice with reference to Rushdie unequivocally.

Nonetheless, this defence and entire exercise of generating opinion remain *aspectical* and ephemeral endeavours. The entire gamut of debate is being reduced or converted to 'individualised freedom' which is different from individual freedom. The absence of freedom comes into prominence not due to real absence of freedom but because a particular individual is involved. Analogously, in the realm of corollary, 'Booker-winning' author Salman Rushdie occupied a very significant space due to his cancellation of visit on the ground of obvious non-cooperation of the government despite his PIO (Person of Indian Origin) status. The focus remained 'big', 'prolific', 'great', 'asset' and 'sublime author' centric. Again, the great opportunity is given a miss to explore why freedom is absent *in toto* in place of un-weaving the causes of individualised freedom.

Individualised freedom needs to be avoided to know the obfuscation of freedom of all. The natural differentiation between two types of freedom, i.e. freedom of especial (individualised freedom) and freedom of all often crop up due to liberal dilemma. Liberal dilemma is the condition when freedom of few is universalised at the expense of all. Ironically, freedom of few is also not protracted when complexity gets unfolded. Therefore, there is liberal bewilderment i.e. how someone's freedom can be suspended.[2]

The liberal dilemma ignores structural constraints. Despite the vagaries and indigenised version of liberalism, as claimed by many, the core problem herein remains the evasion of structural replacement. Apropos the Rushdie affair, what is ignored in the whole debate is the essentiality of problems. The Left and progressive forces across the world are fighting for egalitarian world wherein relationship will not be contingent upon ownership or social ascription. In fact, both factors will be abolished. But this egalitarian world does not come in vacuum. It comes in the form of language. Real struggle gets described in the form of language. One needs to communicate to other through a certain medium. Struggle against real world is also struggle for communicating with the needy and the fellows. The real struggle will have imprint on medium. The message can be mediated as argued by Raymond Williams, Terry Eagleton and others. When real struggle is original and genuine for marginal classes and groups, then medium will also be authentic, stark and tumultuous. Arts, cinema, novels, poetry and so on will have a different, and may be, mediated form. But this language of medium will have to be scathing enough to destabilise the prevalent situation while carrying out the alternative before people. In other words, the essentiality of problems is dealing with the exploitative structure and envisaging the language which will shake the mainstream artefacts.

From the standpoint of essentiality of problems, following questions can be asked foursquarely. But before that, I would like to point out one caveat. Desire for freedom is a different issue from possibility of existence of desired freedom. Desire for 'desired' freedom is commensuration of real struggle and alternative visions. Put differently, can we have real freedom when structures remain exploitative and become more barbaric? This is the second question, i.e. feasibility of existence of desired freedom. To answer this question, we have to understand liberal dilemma. Under the guise of liberalism even in classical liberalism, freedom is avowed. But the problem of liberalism is that it promises freedom but never actualises it. The dichotomy between promises and actualisation gets always prolonged since factors of freedom are monopolised by few. Factors of freedom undoubtedly are material and social power. Freedom cannot be guaranteed when these two factors are centralised and serving the cause of miniscule section of the population.

The opinionated media does not see factors of freedom but focuses on promises of liberalism. But here again is the partiality of gazing. For millions, freedom of expression is a distant dream. The real struggle for them is to acquire the ability to express. Numerous expressions of proletariats, minorities, dalits, women, tribals and others have scantily and calculatedly found spaces. Incessant denial, ignorance and manipulation regarding expression have been the fate of millions. This has been ignored. Underneath the Rushdie affair, freedom is reduced to individual with qualifying integers like best author, award winning, charismatic, widely read and accomplished. But this also does not serve the purpose. If freedom is turned into selective freedom, then condition for freedom is not created because factors of freedom are not liberated or decentralised. Any creative person like actor, novelist, painter – if not critical (might be supportive of the state or at least not a challenger) – cannot be as useful as forces behind accumulation and social immobility. Whenever the state has the opportunity or dilemma to choose forces of accumulation and social repression, and creative people, it opts for the former. This has been missed by 'genuine' liberals and advocates of freedom who remain ignorant of structural causes and rely on the state's promise that all contradictions will be resolved. The state, in a case like this, adopts the method of convergence and repulsion.

Method of Convergence

Contradictory forces do come together sometimes to protract their essence. They cannot tolerate even an iota of emasculation of essence. In this particular context, method of convergence is a way of bringing all fundamentalists together in terms of defending essence of the religion. Method of convergence generates a peculiar condition. The fundamentalists across religions endorse each other's claim on prohibition of even slack interpretation of text or re-portrayal of images. Method of convergence brings back travesty of unity that is unity of fundamentalists endorsing 'their' equal rights of complete insulation from creative interpretation. It means that many, who write, do so for cajoling. There are numerous progressive confrontanist writings and regressive confrontanist writings. The former is without biases and would question all and suggest alternative. The latter writings would find fault selectively and come up with alternative myths. They do not question premise of myth/history but change certain sequences. They flare up the problem.

The state brings inter and intra unity of fundamentalist by 'respecting' their opinion. But it would never tell them that rebuttal is feasible by way of writings. Expression of disagreement is possible through multiple ways but has been utilised in the form of banning. It serves three purposes. First, the state emerges as *messiah* which keeps identitarian circle intact and protects the inside-outside attack on religion. This happens without much effort. Second, the state can keep the contradictions like poverty, dispossession and multifarious subjugation under wrap. Third, there is an attempt to bypass the struggle against the sources of exploitation and subjugation by providing the solace of being 'protector'.

Method of Repulsion

The method of repulsion is an equally retrogressive act. The method of repulsion diminishes the difference between the act and the actor. In other words, if any creation of A is 'wrongful' and 'profane' then s/he is also guilty of blasphemy. At the outset, 'creation' is prohibited but it is not sufficed. S/he is turned into a zealot. Creation can be banned, destroyed or confiscated. Although these options are no longer relevant due to technological development yet it is believed by many. What to do of creators? Since the line between creation and creator is being blurred, creator becomes the centre of attack *ipso facto*. The range of attack against creator stretches from legal battle to incessant abuses and possibly physical injury[3].

The blurred distinction between creator and creation and subsequent attack on latter is not naïve but takes place through covert and overt support. First of all, the state treats it as an irrelevant issue. Thereupon, it is treated as a law and order problem. Moreover, inflictors of promised injuries are never punished despite mushrooming of this brigade. The consequent implications are being self-exiled or leading a life full of battles every day. A glaring example is M.F. Hussain, perhaps finest painter of modern India, who salvaged himself from Hindutva forces through by taking citizenship of Qatar.

Conclusion

The unfortunate aspect of 'unvisit' development would be its remembrance *only* as a curtailment of individualised freedom. Indeed, the entire episode of Rushdie's un-visit suggests following possible reminders. The struggle for collective freedom will only be guarantor of individual freedom. Freedom of expression of all will ensure freedom of each. It does not mean that 'each' freedom is not important. In fact, they are very important, but the problem is that individual freedom cannot be protracted if collective freedom is absent. The reason for absence of collective freedom is structural constraints. Unless structural constraints are done away with, collective freedom, and even for that matter, individual freedom cannot be protracted. The focus on and belief in the promise of liberalism of freedom of expression is ignoring the structural causes which inhibit the freedom of entirety.

NOTES

1. The Rushdie File edited by Lisa Appignanesi and Sara Maitland (Appignanesi & Maitland, 1990) can be referred to understand 'The Author and the Book', 'The Mounting Protest', 'The Khomeinin Fatwa', 'The International Response [United Kingdom, France, Germany, Italy, Norway, Egypt, Canada and United States]' and 'Reflections'.
2. The response of Salman Rushdie, aftermaths the ban of Satanic Verses in India, to then Prime Minister Rajiv Gandhi in 1989 conforms to the tendency and belief of 'universalisation of few'. According to him,

   > The right to freedom of expression is at the very foundation of any democratic society, and at present, all over the world, Indian democracy is becoming something of a laughing stock. When Syed Shahabuddin and his fellow self-appointed guardians of Muslim sensibility say that 'no civilised society' should permit the publication of a book like mine, they have got things backwards. The question raised by the book's banning is precisely whether Indian, by behaving in this somewhat South African fashion, can any more lay claim to the title of a civilised society (Rushdie, 1990: 35).

   The problem of this letter is not that it focuses on right to expression but on the neglect of structural causes. Exclusion of structural factors can be noticed here.

3. Creation–creator distinction has been maintained by many who theoretically and politically do not support Salman Rushdie. Edward Said is one of the important luminaries. Edward Said, after publication of the Satanic Verses, had 'criticised Salman Rushdie for using his intimate knowledge of his community to feed the anti-Muslim prejudices of the West and showing a "lack of loyalty" to it' (Said cited in Parekh, 2000: 159). Nonetheless, he defended him as 'creator' along with other important academicians like Aga Shahid Ali (Hamilton College), Ibrahim Abu-Lughod (Northwestern University), Akeel Bilgrami (Columbia University) and Eqbal Ahmad (Hampshire College) in a letter to The New York Review of Books. The text reads as follows:

   As writers and scholars from the Islamic world, we are appalled by the vilification, book banning and threats of physical violence against Salman Rushdie, the gifted author of Midnight's Children, Shame and The Satanic Verses. This campaign is done in the name of Islam, although none of it does Islam any credit. Certainly Muslims and others are entitled to protest against The Satanic Verses if they feel the novel offends their religion and cultural sensibilities. But to carry protest and debate over into the realm of bigoted violence is in fact antithetical to Islamic traditions of learning and tolerance. We deplore and regret this sort of thing, and we reaffirm our belief in universal principles of rational discussion and freedom of expression (Said, Ali, Abu-Lughod, Bilgrami & Ahmad, 1989).

   Creator and creation distinction is also available in Bhikhu Parekh. For him, protestor and press both were guilty because they focused on person not the book (Parekh, 1990).

2

B.R. Ambedkar, Freedom and Class of Politics

In my opinion, the most reasonable and concrete thing that can be said about the ethical and cultural state is this: every state is ethical in as much as one of its most important functions is to raise the great mass of the population to a particular cultural and moral level, a level (or type) which corresponds to the needs of the productive forces of development, and hence to the interests of the ruling classes. The school as a positive educative function, and the courts as a repressive and negative educative function, are the most important state activities in this sense: but, in reality, a multitude of other so-called private initiatives and activities tend to the same end -initiatives and activities which form the apparatus of the political and cultural hegemony of the ruling classes.

—Antonio Gramsci (Gramsci, 2000: 234)

Cartoon controversy[1] of National Council of Educational Research and Training (NCERT)[2] Political Science book, *Indian Constitution at Work*, has brought forth Janus-faced consequences in India. On the one hand, opinions have oppugned the legitimacy of action over cartoon and on the other hand, notion of B.R. Ambedkar's freedom, which thus far had faced imposed oblivion, has come to fore. It has to be argued categorically that the nature of cartoon cannot be insulated from discussion. Along with, it is equally right that spur-of-the-moment translation of demand into action sans further deliberations turns the action into an inscrutable ploy. Above and beyond merit and demerit of both sides[3], association between Ambedkar's freedom and agency of guarantor and implementer of freedom poses an intricate question. It has to be answered whether ideational freedom of Ambedkar complies with political institution or not. If the political institution does not comply with Ambedkar's freedom, interpretation of act is supplicated.

B.R. Ambedkar and Freedom

One of the authoritative scholars on Ambedkar and dalit movement, Eleanor Zelliot attributes many meanings to Ambedkar ranging from 'inspiration for the educated, hope for the illiterate, threat to the establishment, creator of opportunities for dalits to discomfort for the elites' (Zelliot, 2001: 129-142). The numerous and vivid construal of Ambedkar is not speculative but corporeally rooted for arrival of freedom by way of 'recognition of graded inequality' (Guru, 2002: 41.), 'rejection of humiliation' (Guru, 2009), 'assertion of the human rights' (Keer, 2009: 523) and 'production of new men [and women]' (Kuber, 2001: 11). They are certainly not in existence due to the process of profound production of hagiographic literature. Personification by pontiffs is also not required to discern the idea of freedom in him. Freedom is nomology in his schema. It is the foundational axiom around which connecting parts have been developed.

Freedom being nomological principle in Ambedkar's schema, it has three intrinsic attributes. The first one is freedom from *Chaturvarna*[4]. There are five rules of it. First, society is divided into four classes (Ambedkar uses the term classes in place of group or category). Second, equality is prohibited amongst four classes i.e. graded inequality. Third, there is division of occupations without possibility of 'trespassing'. The fourth rule is debarment of education of shudras. The fifth rule is division of life into four stages i.e.

Brahmancharya (study and education), *Grahasthashram* (living a married life), *Vanaprastha* (serving family ties) and *Sanyasa* (search of God and union with him). The first stage and the last stage were not open for the *shudras* and women (Ambedkar, 2006: 87-89). Ambedkar categorically rejects multi-layered vertical divisions and emphasises on horizontal relations by the state intervention and preferring exogamous marriages over endogamous marriages. Freedom from *Chaturvarna* is freedom of transcendental mobility.

Second attribution confirms the synthesis among liberty, equality, fraternity. There have been invariable construals/ misconstruals of these three values in terms of prioritising one against another two or either one. Indeed, in Ambedkar's outline, freedom encompasses liberty, equality and fraternity. The difference between freedom and liberty is noteworthy. Liberty cannot be synonymised with freedom. Freedom has a bigger circle, and it is the circle of these three components. Freedom remains abortive sans either component. For Ambedkar, liberty encompasses civil liberty (liberty of movement; speech, i.e. thought, reading, writing and discussion; action) and political liberty (making and unmaking government; individuals' right to share in the framing of laws). In the absence of freedom of opinion, the status quo might become stereotyped and most necessary originality is discouraged (Ambedkar, 1987). Ambedkar treated equality as created-equal (Ambedkar, 2009: 45). Created-equal has to be seen in consonance with his critique of Brahmanism and Capitalism. Created-equal should not be treated as mere ascriptive equality but profound equality in eventual life. Fraternity is the necessary treatment to fellow beings as reverence, love and being in unity with her/ him. Moreover, fraternity is not a docile sermon (inactive sermons).

Third attribution is finality of universality of freedom. Ambedkar's recourse to freedom unveils two strategies. At the first level, contextualisation of freedom remained an inalienable theory and its practice. It was reflected on many occasions; for examples, during the All-India Depressed Classes Conference, July 18 and 19, 1942, Ambedkar's advice to dalits (depressed classes) was to 'educate, agitate and organise' (Keer, 2009: 351). Freedom would remain unachievable sans education. The process of education leads to the creation of active agency, self culminates into agitation and finally result into collective organisation. These three are inseparable for activating agency. It is imperative for dalits to be an active agency. The second strategy was combining first with non-ascriptive struggle. Movements against *Khoti* landlord system in 1930s and anti-working class bill (1938), also known as black bill, suggest inclusion of not only freedom issues of 'self-others' but also the attempt to demolish the dichotomy of 'self' and 'other', i.e. your issue and my issue. It was confirmed by him while suggesting that his 'battle is a battle for freedom and reclamation of human personality' (Keer, 2009: 351).

Class of Politics

The aforesaid theory and practice of freedom must become a vantage point to discern Ambedkar's idea of *class of politics*. There is a difference between *political class* and *class of politics*. Political class resembles political society for managing affairs of the government being a representative of people. Partha Chatterjee interprets political society as a group of underclass bargaining with political system particularly during election for their survival (Chatterjee, 2004 & 2011). Ambedkar would differ significantly from this definition of political society. For him, political society *ipso facto* includes people who do not bargain but directly control the state power. The idea is not to bargain but control. Political society in Ambedkar's lexicon is people's power directly or indirectly controlling the government. He did have great deference for the political class as people's power. He himself was part of the Bombay

Legislative Council, the Constituent Assembly and the Indian Parliament; and founded political parties. Eleanor Zelliot opines that behind numerous political activities, Ambedkar had 'a strong, unwavering belief in the power of democratic institutions to bring about social equality' (Zelliot, 1996: 115).

Class of politics is evaluation of politics itself. Class of politics is a methodological tool whereby nature of politics in terms of class–caste–gender is being judged. Political class or people's power remains the desired goal. The quintessence of political class is political power. Highlighting the significance of political power, Ambedkar says that the essence of the distinction between a ruling race and a subject race is exclusion of latter from political power (Ambedkar, 1990a). There is no anathema concerning political class or political power in Ambedkar unlike neo-liberal propagators of shining-India. Politics and being political are enlivening entities. Ambedkar remained sanguine of political class without losing sense of its nature. Class of politics was used by Ambedkar to judge the tenacity and nature of political class. Therefore, the entire issue of representation right from the first round table conference till provision for reservation in the Constitutional Assembly Debate was thoroughly discussed and adopted. Ambedkar was certain of political class/power for the transformation but remained sceptical of prominent leadership about their commitment and desire towards transformation. Class of politics informed him about nature and actuality of political class, not against it.

Asymmetrical Institution

Now the real problem comes to the fore, i.e. how to deal with the political institution or *political class*? *Class of politics* would tell us about the existence of variety of political classes. India has witnessed heterogeneity of a political class. It is utterly wrong to suggest the presence of homogeneity of a political class. Progressive politics has created its own niche. There is nothing like a political class but political classes. It is also true that Indian political institutions have fundamentally been ruled by a particular class due to fragmentation of progressive political class and its inability to mobilise the victim of infamous Indian trio: class, caste and gender.

Judging from Ambedkar's freedom, a particular political class is answerable for graded inequality, synthesis of liberty–equality–fraternity and upholding of universality of freedom. Regarding graded inequality, dalits remain the worst victim of physical annihilation. They are faced not only with humiliation but also with physical annihilation by dominant castes. Liberty, particularly of opinion, is being attempted to be thwarted by introduction of bill, censorship or control in few hands. Pauperisation of people has mocked the idea of equality. Intermittent attempt not to reduce poverty but the poor by introducing/setting cruel criterion is the complete sign of post/neo-liberal methodology wherein appearance becomes 'need and recognition' over essence. Commodity fetish discourse onwards liberalisation has reduced moral worth, an important concern of fraternity, of each as exchangeable commodity. Universality of freedom has been circumscribed to freedom of few who have become beneficiary of the institutions.

Under these circumstances, first, the act of the political institution led by a political class on cartoon controversy owes an explanation. It has to be answered by the defenders of the action as to why does a political ruling class remain silent over gross violation of Amedkar's axioms but suddenly becomes active to protect him. That a particular political class was forced by progressive political class is an untenable position because despite the latter's many attempts, the former has not budged on aforesaid issues which were very close to Ambedkar and are needed for social revolution in India. Second, can any act of defiance or opposition to acts of a political class in and out of institutions be construed as a defiance of political class? This is also an untenable position for the following two reasons. First, opposition to an act is not opposition of political class precisely because nature of an act has its own merits and demerits. Second, exposing the demerits is not deriding the political class. A challenge to an act of a political class is a challenge to the respective group. Asking for interpretation of an act of asymmetrical institution is asking for revelation of class of politics.

NOTES

1. The issue of cartoon removal was called down in the Indian Parliament, made by the legendry cartoonist Shankar Pillai in 1949, from a National Council of Educational Research and Training (NCERT) Book. In this cartoon, B.R. Ambedkar (the architect of the Indian Constitution and revolutionary against untouchability and other oppression) is sitting on a snail and holds a whip. Jawaharlal Nehru also holds a whip and is standing behind the snail and Ambedkar. On the snail's body, the word 'Constitution' is written. It has been stated that original intention of cartoon was to exhibit the slow growth of the Indian Constitution making. However, opponents to this cartoon would say that since Ambedkar belonged to dalit community (ex-untouchable), and holding of a whip by Jawaharlal Nehru behind him as if latter is instructing former in an abusive manner is humiliating.

   On the direction of the Government of India, the Expert Committee/Thorat Panel [comprising Indian Council of Social Science Research's Chairman Prof. S.K. Thorat, Prof. A.S. Narang (IGNOU), Patricia Mukhim (the Editor, Shillong Times), Prof. M.S.S. Pandian (JNU), Abha Malik (Sanskriti School) and Prof. Saroj Yadav (NCERT)] was constituted. The key recommendation of this committee is to do away with cartoons aimed at politicians and bureaucrats. Prof. M.S.S. Pandian submitted a long dissenting note. The thrust of his note is:

   'What's politically incorrect need not be educationally inappropriate'.
2. NCERT is a supreme body to assist and advice the Ministry of Human Resource and Development (MHRD) (earlier it was

known as Ministry of Education), Government of India. Its main task is to, inter alia, prepare school text books ranging from class I to class XII in all subjects. After the defeat of National Democratic Alliance led by the right wing Bhartiya Janata Party (BJP) in General Election of 2004, United Progressive Alliance (UPA-I) formed the government at the centre with the support of the Left Parties. UPA-I revised and removed the earlier text books which were meant for Hindutvas glorification particularly in social sciences. New methods like insertion of coloured pictures and cartoons as a pedagogical tool were made an intrinsic part of the text books.

3. The merit and demerit of both opposing schools have been argued. The merit of inclusionary argument, those who are in favour of intactness of the book and the cartoon, lies in defending the book. Normative reading of Political Science books of NCERT would suggest that they are relatively more inclusive than earlier ones. Their only demerit is their square rejection of non-negotiability of the text books. The merit of exclusionary argument, those arguments which are favouring expunging of the cartoon/s, is vociferous questioning of normal. However, they have suffered from two serious demerits. The first demerit is the handing out of the space to the state which exists between the translation of action and actions. Immediate translation of demand into action by the state is certainly not innocuous action. Second, personification of Ambedkar by pontiffs by way of equating him with God would not only dump the immense criticality generated by Ambedkar but would also weaken the struggle against *dharmik* salvation. [For more on it see (Rai, 2012b)]
4. Hindu society has been divided into four groups based on ascriptive identity.

3

Familial Politics, Familiar Political Class and Democracy

The recognition of the existence of a governing class as a fundamental and a crucial fact confronting democracy and self-government is the only safe and realistic approach to those who wish for democracy and self-government to come into their own. It is a fatal blunder to omit to take account of it in coming to a conclusion as to whether in a free country will be the privilege of the governing class only or it will be the possession of all.

—B.R. Ambedkar (Ambedkar, 2002: 134)

Democracy provides an incessant opportunity for its evaluation. Electoral contestation of Dimple Yadav in the by-election of Kannauj Lok Sabha constituency (Uttar Pradesh, 2012), a seat vacated by the Chief Minister of Uttar Pradesh, can be one context of reassessment. This cannot be construed as 'mere' news. It has, like previous ones, serious multiple implications on democracy. Being the wife of the incumbent Chief Minister of Uttar Pradesh Akhilesh Yadav is her reconfirmed and reasserted political identity. The mainstream media had presented and boasted it as 're-coronation' of Dimple Yadav. Her electoral contestation has to be termed as re-coronation because her first attempt was scuttled by Raj Babbar in Firozabad Lok Sabha constituency by-election (2009). This time (2012), all parties had failed to field candidates against her thus paving the way for her unopposed election. Therefore, in this phase of coronation in democracy (a discrete phenomenon in South Asia), revision of democratic values becomes an imminent priority.

Democracy, Participation and Participants

Democracy invites multiple connotations and pages of political theory texts are a great signpost and testimony to it. I will confine or construct two arguments, as discussed in the introduction, on which the desired democratic theory must function. The first can be construed as 'democracy as participation'. The second entails 'democracy as realisation of being participants'. Of course, democracy as participation and realisation of being participants are being derived and shaped by larger mission, vision and ambition of people's inspiration and struggle. Any democratic theory remains deficient if it does not take account of people's struggle. The procedural and structural eulogies are not sufficient conditions; they might be a reference point. The purpose here is to evaluate the functioning of liberal democracy in India.

One of the important components of liberal democracy is party politics. Though party politics, political transformation and electoral politics have become a vantage point to understand Indian democracy, they remain inept due to the omission of a fundamental question that is the democratisation of political parties. Democratisation of means of democracy is a vital question. Democratisation of political parties is very important due to two factors. The symptom of political parties is the symptom of Indian democracy. The first factor is participation. Even liberal democracy would be deprived of being democracy if 'one person, one vote' is not operational. Before this, necessary participation in political parties becomes a crucial task. This compulsory participation in political parties ensures greater democratisation. The second factor is realisation of being participants which ensures that values are allocated to them while combating discrimination.

The collective aspiration of people gets transformed in parliamentary democracy via political parties. It does not mean that people do suspend all other modes of democratic expression/endeavour. But certainly political parties are one of the means. The constituency of each political party is a heterogeneous amalgam led by a core group or groups. Even then, the respective political party has to take account of heterogeneous groups. Even one caste in India is heterogeneous in nature on the basis of sociological account and empirical reality. It has to address a heterogeneous claim.

Understanding the structure of democracy is crucial. The structure gives ample clues whether it is participatory or not. It can also be deciphered whether the principle of realisation of being participants does function or not. Many means of Indian democracy have violated the fundamental values of democracy that is message of inclusiveness and practice of egalitarianism.

Familial Politics and its Phases

Familial politics is the politics of incessant succession within democracy in and by political parties. A difference could be elaborated between familial politics and dynasty politics. Connotations of dynasty politics exhibit the phenomenon of successive rulers from the broad family, sometimes denoted by surnames or acquired title. It is a long-term phenomenon. Formation of ruling family or dynasty politics is itself an 'epochal' phenomenon. Familial politics can be started any time, and members are drawn from nuclear family. Familial politics is a modern phenomenon. It is small in scope and narrow in drawing leadership. Apart from these small differences, impact and functioning of dynasty politics and familial politics remain more or less similar.

Pradeep Chibber explains three factors as to why some parties are dynastic. 'First, the party should not have an independent party organization. Second, the party should not rely on an independent civil society association that will mobilize voters for the party. The third condition suggests that funds for the party must be collected and disbursed centrally' (Chibber, 2011: 15). According to him, '...the presence of dynastic parties leads to greater party system instability and also to a representation deficit' (Chibber, 2011: 15). Besides, historical–social values cannot be underestimated. The idea of *paterfamilias* in the family gets extended into society in the form of *paterfamilias* family in wider realm. The unquestioned legitimacy acquired by *paterfamilias* in the family due to class–caste–patriarchy is being used for furthering the *paterfamilias* family in the form of familial politics.

Familial politics did not come without relation adjectives which are centralities of families. The Gangetic belt has invented and practiced the notion of *Bhaiya-Bhabhi—Bahu-Chacha-Chachi-Mama-Mami* tradition. Eastern India is now frontrunner of *'dada'* and *'didi'* tradition. The south has witnessed the *'Anna'* tradition. The western India has kith and kin tradition along with continuous presence of *'maharaja'* and *'maharani'*. Mainstream *status quo* parties have used aforesaid practice as a guarantor of clinching electoral victory in democracy. There have broadly been three phases of familial politics in India.

The first phase (1919-1977) encompasses both pre-independence and post-independence India. Motilal Nehru was made the president of Indian National Congress (INC) during Amritsar (1919) and Calcutta (1928) sessions. Thereafter, Jawaharlal Nehru became the president in Lahore (1929), Lucknow (1936), Faijpur (1937), New Delhi (1951), Hyderabad (1953) and Kalyani (1954) sessions. Meanwhile, a key member of the family, Vijaya Lakshmi Pandit had the opportunity to become the nation's first female minister (1937-1939 and 1946-1947) from the United Provinces. Except from May 27, 1964 to January 24, 1966, the Prime Minister post remained with Nehru–Gandhi (Jawaharlal Nehru

August 15, 1947-May 27, 1964 and Indira Gandhi January 24, 1966 -24 March 1977) family. The INC led by Nehru–Gandhi family won 74.43% seats in 1951-1952, 75.10% seats in 1957, 73% seats in 1962, 54.42% seats in 1967 and 68% seats in the 1971 general elections.

There are five important aspect of this phase. First, familial politics, barring a few exceptions, was confined to the INC. Second, regional leaders in the INC had started allocating important positions to their kith and kin. It was broadly confined to the states. Third, this was depicted by Rajni Kothari as 'the Congress System' synonymising country's political stability and democracy (Kothari, 1964: 1161-1173). The fourth aspect is more important. There was still deep resentment over familial politics. Almost all the non-Congress parties had opposed it. Fifth, the phase had put a solid foundation of familial politics which can be verified by political presence and activism of Sanjay Gandhi in the INC. A thing to be noticed is that with Sanjay Gandhi, a term like 'extra-constitutional authority' came into being. According to Granville Austin, Indira Gandhi 'was also to be encircled by the inner ring of her son Sanjay and his henchmen—who were referred to as the "coterie" or "caucus" and as the "extra-constitutional authority"—often acting in her stead. His advocacy of the Emergency and his role in preparing arrest lists before it has been described' (Austin, 2008: 325). Nikhil Chakravarty maintains that 'she allowed Sanjay to have a team of his own, and this developed into a real caucus'[1] (cited in Austin, 2008: 325).

Familial politics faced a stiff challenge during the second phase (1977-1980). For the first time, the INC was out of power from the centre and two non-Congress candidates became the Prime Minister. Indira Gandhi and Sanjay Gandhi were defeated. The INC won only 35% of the total seats. In other words, non-familial political parties won 65% of the total seats. However, the effectiveness of the Nehru family was not reduced in the INC. Due to internecine development in the Janata Party, the struggle against familial politics did not go far.

The third phase (1980-1989) began with the exhibition of the INC dominance in 1980 and 1984 Lok Sabha elections. In both elections, the Congress had 69% and 81% of the total seats , respectively. The post of Prime Minister and president of the INC remained with the Nehru family (Indira Gandhi, Rajiv Gandhi in 1983 and 1985). With this phase, familial politics started getting legitimacy.

The fourth stage (since 1989) has a new form of democracy metamorphosed by familial politics. Familial politics is not limited to the INC, now. Interestingly, many political parties who owed their existence to anti-familial politics have become the den of familial politics. There is symmetry and asymmetry between the INC and other political parties. The symmetry is in the sense that the INC (Motilal Nehru, Jawaharlal Nehru, Indira Gandhi, Sanjay Gandhi, Rajiv Gandhi, Sonia Gandhi and Rahul Gandhi), Dravida Munnettra Kazhagam (DMK) (Karunanidhi, Stalin, Alagiri and Kanimojhi), Rashtriya Janata Dal (RJD) (Lalu Prasad and Rabri Devi), Indian National Lokdal (INL) (Devi Lal, Om Prakash Chautala and Abhay Chautala), National Conference (NC) (Sheikh Abdullah, Farooq Abdullah and Omar Abdullah), Shiromani Akali Dal (SAD) (Prakash Singh Badal and Sukhbir Singh Badal), Peoples' Democratic Party (PDP) (Mufti Mohammad Sayeed and Mehbooba Mufti), Biju Janata Dal (BJD) (Biju Patnaik and Navin Patnaik), Samajwadi Party (SP) (Mulayam Singh Yadav, Ram Gopal Yadav, Akhilesh Yadav and Dimple Yadav), Rashtriya Lok Dal (RLD) (Charan Singh, Ajit Singh and Jayant Singh), National Congress Party (NCP) (Sharad Pawar and Supriya Phule), Shiv Sena (SS) (Bal Thackeray and Uddhav Thackeray), Telugu Desam Party (TDP) (N T. Rama Rao and Chandrababu Naidu), Janata Dal (Secular) (H.D. Deve Gowda and H.D. Kumaraswamy), Haryana Janhit Congress (HJC) (Bhajan Lal and Kuldeep Bishnoi) and Jharkhand

Mukti Morcha (JMM) (Shibu Soren and Hemant Soren) are controlled by families. Out of these sixteen parties, three are national parties and the rest are state parties. They have 57% of the total Lok Sabha seats.

According to Patrick French, the fifteenth Lok Sabha (2009-2014) comprises 28.6% (156/545) Members of Parliament (MPs) from political dynasties. Five most hereditary parties are RLD (total MPs: 5; linked with political families: 5 (100.0%)), NCP (total MPs: 9; linked with political families: 7 (77.8%)), BJD (total MPs: 14; linked with political families: 6 (42.9%)), INC (total MPs: 208; linked with political families: 78 (37.5%)) and BSP (total MPs: 21; linked with political families: 7 (33.3%)). Percentage of hereditary MPs by age is even more shocking: below 30 years: 100%; between 31 and 40 years: 65%; for 41–50 years: 36.8 %; in age group of 51–60, 61–70, 71–80 and above 81, respective percentages were 20.6, 16.4, 10.5 and 0 (French, 2011: 116–119).

From the asymmetry point of view, the fundamental difference between the INC and other political parties is that the former has two types of families. First family is the Nehru family. Second type of families come from the states wherein the first generation was politically active. These states are Madhya Pradesh (Scindia), Uttar Pradesh (Kamla Pati Tripathi and Jitendra Prasad), Maharashtra (S.B. Chavan), Rajasthan (Rajesh Pilot family), Punjab (the former royal family) and Haryana (Hooda and Jindal family). It has been publicised by the name of *Yuvavad*. NCP comes closer to this configuration of the INC where other than Sharad Pawar's family, P.A. Sangma's family [before expulsion from the NCP] used to have sway over the party while occupying all the important posts in the state of Meghalaya.

Familial Politics and Familiar Political Class

Democracy as participation demands that there has to be participation without discrimination. Rules of party are different from stated/unstated discriminatory practices.

Democracy as realisation of being participants demands that each participant feels the actualisation or struggle towards actualisation of equal beings. In context of India, even the fundamentals of liberal democracy are violated. There are two violations; first, from liberal democracy standpoint and second, from equal being perspective.

The first violation is curbing the democracy as participation. Demand for being elected is sought on the grounds of familial politics. Election after election, it has now become a norm by conformist parties to field the candidates on the premise of familial politics principle in place of democratic principle. The familial principle / representation is not principled on democratic theory / representation. The election / re-election does not serve the purpose of democratic ambitions.

In the context of Indian democracy, familial politics generally gets more boon in by-elections than general elections. General elections sometimes may provide the scope to follow the democratic principle that is a homogenous reflection of people in political structure of the party. It has been observed that 'by-elections' provide scope for pursuance of familial politics. Often, by-elections take place due to the sudden demise or resignation on some unavoidable grounds. The succession line draws from family of the concerned individuals.

Constitutionally, familial politics, which also can be termed as Indian 'democratic' succession, is still democratic by way of procedural definition of democracy. However, this not only bypasses the gist of democracy but also produces three negative consequences. The first negative outcome is the abdication of repulsion against familial politics due to its repetition, and also due to brazen celebration as coronation by media and respective political party / parties. The second negative consequence is the production or proliferation of a familiar political class. A familiar political class resolves inner contradictions and starts operating homogeneously. Herein, attempt towards alternatives gets weakened. Third, democracy as participation gets also shrunk due to absence of democracy and democratic practices.

Moreover, there is a severe consequence on realisation of being participants' front. Realisation of being participants in people's democracy is contingent on mitigation of discrimination towards freedom and material availability. The consequence is a theoretical one whereby justification of discrimination might percolate. Since familial politics is based on birth, in principle it cannot oppose the discriminations which are birth-based. In modern India, three forms of discriminations can easily be identified. The first is caste-based discrimination. The method of domination by dominant castes over dalits and other weaker sections are drawn from the legitimacy on the basis of ascriptive superiority. The second is economic discrimination. It is also interesting to see how 'class' is sometimes linked with the birth. The economic discrimination has quadrupled during neoliberalism. There are two important conditions of neoliberalism which is expanding since 1991. They are private property and freedom to do a contract. But more than these two conditions, necessarily property transformation within the family is another hallmark. The greatest beneficiaries of private property are those who are born in the family. Neoliberalism underlines the accumulative endeavour and right to contract to these proprietary people. Thirdly, patriarchy is also linked with birth. The discrimination meted out to the women is due to the body which is also birth related. The accelerated discrimination of the three forms gets increased primarily because familial politics-led-governments are in the helm of affairs. Since, familial politics is itself a birth-related phenomenon, it becomes almost impossible for any politics or government to fight against any discrimination which is linked with birth. Emergence of a familiar political class stops the possibility of fighting against discrimination due to arrival of unanimity amongst them for ruling and *status quo*.

The familial politics and familiar political class can be countered when participation and realisation of being participants principle can be forced for achieving people's democracy against fragmented democracy. Indeed, it is needless to say that people's struggle comes first before any other means.

NOTES

1. In this regard, Sudipta Kaviraj makes succinct explanations. He states that

   Instead of effort at building the party, Congress went through a curious policy of induction of members into the Youth Congress, providing a platform for the rise of Sanjay Gandhi. This not merely led to the well-known unconstitutional uses of power and irrational excesses of the family planning and beautification drives, which naturally fell most heavily on the poorest. It also carried to its extreme the internal reallocation of power within the Congress elite, leading to the gradual decline of the group of more professional advisers around Indira Gandhi. This meant not only an increasing arbitrariness but also loss of consistency, for midway during the Emergency, the government started discussing the advantages of a more conservative form of economic policy. Under normal conditions of democracy, political initiatives, when they show unpopular or dysfunctional consequences, make for their own abandonment. In an authoritarian regime such dysfunctionalities could continue unchecked; for it is inconceivable that any political regime would have continued with the excesses of the sterilisation drive or could have been so uniformed or insensitive towards popular opinion. Authoritarianism made the government behave more ignorantly (Kaviraj, 1986: 1704).

4

Dalits, Globalisation and Economism

> *There are in my view two enemies which the workers of this country have to deal with. The two enemies are Brahmanism and Capitalism.*
>
> —B.R. Ambedkar, *The Times of India*, February 14, 1938

The relationship of dalits and globalisation has been construed in many ways. This chapter proposes that interpretations centring on mere economism have profoundly eclipsed various facets of this relationship. 'Economic' construal entails that not only the defenders of globalisation have found its *sui generis* aspect only in economic-interlinking of nation states and societies but the oppositional forces have also zeroed in on perforating sovereign economic structure of the nation state due to globalisation. In the case of defenders, this is a matter of selective choice whereby they can push forward their subtle but not so subtle agenda.

Nevertheless, for the oppositional and alternative forces, this is nothing but solecism. This invites an explication. Opposition to globalisation (especially in the context of class and identity sense) through merely economic argument per se has been met by the defenders with 'prosperity syndrome', i.e. exhibition of quadrupling gross domestic product, growth rate, emergence of exclusive artefacts like malls and multiplexes. Prosperity syndrome deliberately creates a few elites across the sections to celebrate 'economism'. In this context, for oppositional and alternative forces, it becomes difficult to reveal the real effect of globalisation on dalits and others.

Therefore, there is a need to look beyond this unilinear interpretation. In the context of globalisation where prosperity syndrome occupies the debate, this chapter endeavours to discuss participation and realisation of being participants for dalits.

Explaining Four Caveats

This chapter claims at the outset that four caveats have to be underlined to discern the relationship between dalits and globalisation. First is to abandon the 'binaries.' For 'defenders' of globalisation *vis-à-vis* dalits, the binary is present in the following ways: the argument that so far the state has not done anything for dalits versus the argument that globalisation would do the required; Caste Capitalism versus Casteless Capitalism; Caste Bourgeoisie versus Dalit Bourgeoisie; Openness versus Closeness; American Companies versus Indian Companies; American Democracy versus Indian Democracy; Availability of Goods versus Scarcity of Goods; Restricted Consumptions versus Liberated Consumptions and so on. The severest deficit of the binary analysis is the negation of a slew of issues like exploitation and presence and role of structure in relational manner like inter linkages of various exploitative structures and their working in concert. At best, it in turn becomes a reaction to the existing theories. The issues picked up by them are important but solutions end up as mere appendages in the form of reaction to the existing theories and practices. And this does not lead to transgression of 'other theories/realities' and complete analysis. In a nutshell, the binary analysis begins and ends with reaction in place of transcendence.

The second caveat is the rejection of 'referential' treatment of dalit discourse. Referential treatment entails that there has been an advent of arguments in defence of globalisation, and it is referred as 'globalisation for dalits' without exhibiting the tenets of dalits' discourse and evaluation from its perspective. Actually, the evaluation of globalisation has been done thoroughly from neo-liberal perspective under the influence of binary analysis, and there is complete absence of analysis from the perspective of dalit discourse. The defenders never take pain to approach the argument from within the dalit discourse rather than impose it from outside and term it as a great emancipator.

The third caveat is the rejection of 'preferential' treatment to 'sovereignty' over participation and realisation of being participants. It could be termed as an 'internal' critique of Marxist writings and activism concerning globalisation. Concerning globalisation, the issue of sovereignty occupies an indomitable aspect in Marxist terrain. The sovereignty of the nation state is extremely vital and is needed due to various reasons: defending the nation state to impede the juggernaut of the globalisation and also forming the coalition of equal nation states in concert against the bigger threat along with the sustenance of decision-making ability. The analysis from this vantage point is significant but not complete due to omission of the issue of participation and realisation of being participants and its linkages with globalisation. The sovereignty of the nation state and participation and realisation of being participants occupy a different sphere altogether. As far as the 'external' aspect is concerned, both 'sovereignty' aspect and participation and realisation of being participants share the common podium because in the absence of sovereignty of the nation states, participation and realisation of being participants would not exist. Additionally, it is also possible that in the 'presence' of sovereign nation state, participation and realisation of being participants may not be functional. Moreover, in the absence of sovereignty, certain classes and castes would benefit because globalisation needs alliance of dominant social forces in each country. The sovereignty perspective while highlighting sovereignty brilliantly of the nation state has more or less bypassed the 'internal' factor that is the functioning of participation and realisation of being participants under the influence of globalisation. The analysis of globalisation is vital and becomes complete only when it takes both factors into cognisance: 'sovereignty' to discern the nation state and 'participation and realisation of being participants ' to explore the sovereignty of deprived sections in various aspects.

The fourth and the last caveat is the straightaway rejection of coalescing modernity with globalisation. This is important due to eulogisation of globalisation as the arrival of modernity in the form of globalisation. Coalescing modernity with globalisation is evident in various works, especially in Arjun Appadurai's work *Modernity at Large: Cultural Dimensions of Globalization* (1996) wherein 'imagination' has been celebrated as social force which is creating both identity and energies to replace the nation state which is unlikely to exist anymore. Globalisation has goaded this process through mass migration and electronic mediation (Appadurai, 1996).

The justification of globalisation for the creation of imagination and terming it as 'spread of modernity' is misconstrued due to a variety of reasons. Modernity can be defined as an arena where a slew of inquiries take place through explanation. Modernity is the enabling factor for billions of people who have been deprived and subjugated in the name of orthodoxy, superstition and heavenly orders. Globalisation is a distinct phenomenon. The buzzword in globalisation is 'integration' not 'inquiry.' Modernity enables the people to question whereas globalisation focuses on acceptance of 'integration.' At best, globalisation can be described as a process of modernisation. The process of modernisation that is globalisation also, cannot be termed as modernity. The difference between the two is that one can be modernised without being an imbiber of modernity. In other words, availability of various consumer goods, exchange of technologies and usage of similar goods across the globe nowhere suggests that modernity has arrived because modernity is not at all about consumption of goods in linear ways or imbibing a linear cultural practice, but it is an outlook based on the explanation of various processes through scientific ways. Moreover, terming globalisation as modernity escapes the question of exploitation in the name of integration and the motive behind it. The accumulation of resources in the name of globalisation needs a certain explanation which is inexplicable if it is termed as modernity because modernity is not all about accumulation but is also based on inquiry.

Economism/*a la mode* Economic Integration

Globalisation has primarily been defended by the integrators who either fathom the emancipatory virtues out of it or expect its 'would be' fruitions. The fruitions get explicated through the economic integration especially in the realm of political and social integration. Economic integration, as integrationists claim, vouches for the elevation of the world politically and socially.

The economic integration, besides economic prosperity, constitutes the fulcrum of political and social elevation. Put differently, political and social integration and the resultant elevation is not feasible without economic integration. Locating the debate concerning dalits, it has been averred that economic integration not only brings economic prosperity for dalits but also brings relatively more political partaking and social elevation.

Defending Globalisation for New Turn

Globalisation for dalits has been defended for new turn. New turn is the offshoot of globalisation and encompasses 'caste withering' (Prasad, 2004) thereby escaping 'hunger and humiliation' (Chandra Bhan Prasad cited in Sengupta, 2008); opportunity to possess material goods thus entering into middle class basket and challenging 'Upper Caste Consumer Club' (Prasad, 2009a) and replacement of caste capitalism (Prasad, 2009b). Moreover, consumption patterns of dalits in Uttar Pradesh (based on the survey of everyday consumable items in the eastern block and the western block) in the market reform era have standardised and become more accessible (Kapur, Prasad, Pritchett & Babu, 2010: 39-49).

The Bhopal Document echoes similar resonances (The Bhopal Document, 2002). The Bhopal Document categorically praises the American democracy: 'American society is now an enthusiastic advocate and practitioner of equal opportunity, affirmative action and diverse and in sharing the national prosperity' (The Bhopal Document, 2002: 67). The aforesaid process has received accolade and depicted as 'In Search of a Bourgeoisie: Dalit Politics Enters a New Phase' (Nigam, 2002a: 1190-1193), 'Rashtravadi Chintan Se Pare' (beyond the nationalist thinking) (Nigam, 2002b: 397-403) and 'New Economies of Desire' (Menon and Nigam, 2007: 83-102). '[T]he policies and programmes set out in the BD [Bhopal Document] constituted a break with the past and moved the Dalit Agenda beyond the limited confines of the traditional framework of reservation and the paradigm of social justice in which it has been struck for some time' (Pai, 2012: 112).

New turn is justified because dalits are not very much hurt due to the weakening of the nation state; dalits are not worried about globalisation per se but share therein. They are afraid that in the name of unity for the struggle against globalisation, their own struggle could be asked to be suspended (Nigam, 2002b: 397-403). [T]he new economies of desire include the explosion of a series of new aspirations: the celebration of capitalism by sections of the most oppressed, especially by [d]alits' (Nigam, 2002b: 83). 'The initial years of the neo-liberal regimes were thus spent by

[d]alit intellectuals in mobilizing for "defending the public sector" and "opposing globalization". This was clearly a lost battle from the very beginning, as it is patently clear that nowhere in the world has it been possible to keep up such an extent of governmental intervention in the economy under the new conditions' (Nigam, 2002b: 97). Moreover the arguments state that '[f]or dalits, it is easier to negotiate with foreign capitalists, free they are from the ideology of the caste, which no Indian is capable of being' (Nigam, 2002b: 98).

Furthermore, any sceptical look at the relationship between dalits and globalisation has been summarily rejected because '[b]eing "anti-globalisation" has become the current standard of political correctness. Those upholding the slogan are reluctant to give it up. When it is argued that "globalisation" as such has simply a technological social meaning, is inevitable, and has certain good aspects (all of which the anti-globalisers find hard to deny), they retreat to "opposing imperialist globalisation", or (which is again a different thing) "opposing neo-liberal globalisation..." ' (Omvedt, 2005: 4881). The '...problem with the "anti-LPG" (Liberalisation, Privatisation, Globalisation) position is and has been for some time, that there are missing links, unproved statements and open contradictions in the arguments people are making. For example, one hears "the market is spreading everywhere". But the two statements are contradictory. If the market is spreading, this has to mean that purchasing power is in some way expanding. People have to be getting at least enough employment to buy what is coming onto the market. Otherwise, if poverty, unemployment, etc, are really increasing, the expansion of the market will hit limits and stop'[1] (Omvedt, 2005: 4882). Furthermore, '...reform years coincide with the rise of [d]alit politicians, and that both factors may have contributed to a rise in confidence among Dalits' (Abhijit Banerjee cited in Sengupta, 2008).

Globalisation, Need Principle and Necessity Principle

The defence of globalisation is very much grounded in the theoretical underpinning of globalisation, i.e. 'the need principle' through negating the necessity principle. The need principle envisages and endorses the availability of myriad resources through negotiation. The availability of resources is not *ipso facto* in terms of natural availability to the people. The 'need' is the underlying principle which means the value of resources is omniscient for everyone. The ability to acquire the resources would take place through negotiation in the realm of market. A market is a place where various people are equipped with the ability to negotiate amongst each other and acquire the resources. In other words, the resources are available to those who could negotiate best with their available ability, thereby acquiring the right over resources.

Conversely, the necessity principle avows the undeniable economic rights which would be protracted by participation and realisation of being participants for the invalidation of exploitation. Put differently, there are resources intrinsically linked with life; therefore these are non-negotiable. Since these resources are non-negotiable, it becomes obligatory in nature on the part of the government to protract the delivery of resources to the people. Participation and realisation of being participants entail the responsibility of the elected representative towards the people to ensure the continuance of economic rights and dignified existence. In a way, democratic and economic rights and dignified existence establish dialectical relationship. The effective functioning of participation and realisation of being participants is *sine qua non* for ensuring the availability of economic rights and dignified life thereby becoming mandatory rights to do away with symmetrical inclusion and asymmetrical exclusion.

Put differently, the defenders of globalisation exhibit exuberance of globalisation per se which means inherently the avowal of need, or the construction, of globalisation. The celebration of globalisation itself evinces the arrival of need principle which felt suffocated during the welfare state regimes. Although the welfare state was not necessarily the ultimate destination and designation of progressive forces, it had not abdicated the responsibility to fulfil the necessity principle due to mounting pressure and struggle of the people.

Etymologically and logically, endorsement of globalisation is the recognition of the need principle due to envisioning the world as *the global*. The 'world' represents geographical landscape while the 'global' is an active and assertive endeavour. The 'ism' of the 'global' constitutes one aspect of the need principle.

The defence of the global and need principle can be traced differently in Adam Smith's 'invisible hand' (market is the panacea of all conundrums which operates under the veil of ignorance; 'neutrality' is the key word of market)[2] (Smith, 2003; Rothschild, 1992 & 1994; Hull, 1997; Smith, 1998; Waterman, 2002; Hollander, 1911). For Friedrich Hayek, the institutions of private property, contract, and consent, embedded in a system of general rules that protect these institutions, are crucial not only in mobilising incentives but also in ensuring that economic actors are able to utilize their individual knowledge of time and place in making decisions in such a way that their plans may be realized. These institutions Hayek cites are precisely the institutions of liberalism—private property and freedom of contract protected under a rule of law (Boettke, 2006: 63). Robert Nozick 'argues that individuals in the state of nature, in trying to improve their position, will perform actions which will eventually bring about a minimal state, although no one intended this, or perhaps even thought about the creation of a state' (Wolff, 1991: 42).

Of late, the global had been packaged in the form of 'integration' and 'deterritorialization'. 'The globalization... has one overarching feature-integration' (Friedman, 2000: 8). '[I]t is the inexorable integration of markets, nation-states and technologies never witnessed before—in a way that is enabling individuals, corporations and nation states to reach around the world farther, faster, deeper, cheaper than ever before' (Friedman, 2000: 9). 'The driving idea behind globalisation is free-market capitalism—the more you let market forces rule and the more you open your economy to free trade and competition, the more efficient and flourishing your economy will be. Globalisation means the spread of free-market capitalism to virtually every country in the world. Therefore, globalisation also has its own set of economic rules, rules that revolve around opening, deregulating and privatizing your economy, in order to make it more competitive and attractive to foreign investment' (Friedman, 2000: 9). Herein,

> Deterritorialization, in general, is one of the central forces of the modern world because it brings laboring populations into the lower-class sectors and spaces of relatively wealthy societies, while sometimes creating exaggerated and intensified sense of criticism of attachment to politics in the home-state... At the same time, deterritorialization creates new markets for film companies, art impresarios, and travel agencies, which thrive on the need of the deterritorialized population for contact with its homeland (Appadurai, 2000: 37-38).

> The idea of deterritorialization may also be applied to money and finance, as money managers seek the best markets for their investments, independent of national boundaries (Appadurai, 2000: 49).

The justification of deterritorialization is based on following postulations: evidences do not suggest that the Third World countries were made poorer due to the creation of a single world economy and market; economic dependence is vital; colonialism produced good (in terms of transition) and bad (being an obstacle to growth) effects; tangible benefits offered by the international trade has been accepted willingly by the third world societies and capitalist relations implicit in trade need to be extended throughout the economy; the commodity production and export has to lead to the industrialisation to break the Malthus obstacle of limited land and the obstacle of an elastic and erratic commodity market; and substantial part of manufacturing sector becoming internationally competitive can produce sustained growth produced by industrialisation (Fieldhouse, 1999). It has had positive impact on poverty, child labour, women's rights, democracy, wage and labour standards and the environment (Bhagwati, 2004).

The global encapsulates following features: spread of international trade in goods and services; migration of people between countries or services; migration of people between countries or regions; exchange of money and means of payment on increasing scale across countries or regions; flow of capital from one country to another to help produce goods and services; flow of finance (not necessarily linked to the production of goods and services) between different countries; emergence of TNCs engaged in the activities listed above; international trade in technology; spread of print and electronic media; and growth in international trade and production of services of all kinds like shipping, insurance, banking, finance and healthcare (Bagchi, 1999: 3219-3230).

The second aspect is the 'final shape-up': denudation of constrains is the final desire. In other words, the 'ism' of the global becomes possible when the constraints are circumvented. The confluence of active and assertive endeavours (the global) on the one hand and circumvention of constraints on the other hand form globalisation. The vantage point of the global and circumvention of constraint decides the kind of globalisation. The need principle's vantage point is to envisage the global market and do away with all obfuscation concerning it. Therefore the celebration of globalisation is not only the accolade of the global market but also the demise of sources of obfuscation. Owing to this, liberalisation is an intrinsic aspect of globalisation.

> The essence of liberalisation is that economic management should be left to the market. The prices determined by the interaction of demand and supply forces, whether they be for commodities, labour power, capital, land, or foreign exchange, should be flexible in either direction and should be capable of clearing the market. The resulting allocation of resources, commodities, labour power, foreign currency, etc. would be optimal and efficient, while any deviation from it would entail avoidable social costs. In order to ensure that markets are allowed to undertake their jobs, all controls and regulations, as also measures that constitute barriers to entry, should be done away with (Balassa cited in Dasgupta, 2005: 20-21).

It follows from this that the state should take a back seat in economic matters (Dasgupta, 2005: 21).

Liberalisation is followed by privatisation. Globalisation does not occur in a vacuum however. Its corrosive impact on democratic governance is being hastened by a cognate ideology of privatisation that is prevalent both in the international scene and within the countries whose economies are being globalised. Privatisation is an ideology that shapes democracy by attacking public power, by arguing that markets can do everything government once did better than government and with more freedom for citizens. Privatisation within nation and states opens the way for the deregulation of markets and in turn facilitates globalisation of the economy. It softens up citizens to accept the decline of political institutions and tries to persuade them that they will be better off and more 'free' that way. As an ideology, it insists that government is about illegitimate public power and calls for the substitution of private power, which is simply assumed, without any argument, to be legitimate (Barber, 2001: 303).

The Global, Denudation and Implications

The global and its working (denudation) were envisaged through the original Washington Consensus. The focus was on fiscal discipline, reorientation of public expenditures, tax reform, financial liberalisation, unified and competitive exchange rates, trade liberalisation, openness to foreign direct investment (FDI), privatisation, deregulation and secure property rights. The augmented Washington Consensus also includes legal/political reform, regulatory institutions, anti-corruption, labour market flexibility, WTO agreements, financial codes and standards, 'prudent' capital account opening, non-intermediate exchange rate regimes, social safety nets and Poverty reduction. The Washington Consensus was followed by the Washington Security Agenda which has following features: hegemonic order through dominance, flexible multilateralism or unilateralism where necessary, pre-emptive and preventive use of force; security focus (geopolitical and, secondarily, geoeconomic, collective organization where pragmatic' (UN, NATO), otherwise reliance on US military and political power); leadership (the US and its allies); and aims (making world safe for freedom and democracy and globalizing American rules and justice) (Held, 2005: 35-36) .

Prabhat Patnaik has listed five implications. 'First, there is a tremendous globalization of capital in the form of finance, so much so that trade-related financial flows account just about 2 per cent of total cross-border financial flows. Second, notwithstanding sharp increases in the direct foreign investment (DFI) flows internationally, their total magnitude still remains comparatively small; they still have not broken free from the situation where the north invests largely within the north; and even within the south they tend to come only to those countries which have high levels of domestic savings anyway... [W]hat we have witnessed so far is globalization of capital-as-finance but not globalization of capital-in-production' (Patnaik, 2003: 19). 'Third, this tremendous financial fluidity has undermined the ability of the nation state to intervene in the economy to maintain high levels of activity' (Patnaik, 2003: 19). 'Fourth, notwithstanding the differences among the advanced capitalist countries on numerous issues, and their rivalries in matters of trade, the present conjuncture is marked on the whole by a far greater degree of unity among them than has been the case over the last hundred years (except the post-war situation when there was a sort of artificial unity imposed by US 'super-imperialism' upon the vanquished and the rest of the victors of the war alike). The unity, in turn, owes not a little to the fluidity of finance which has attenuated the scope for the activities of the nation-state' (Patnaik, 2003: 20). 'Fifth, this fluidity of finance represents globalization in a double sense, not only in the sense that finance flows everywhere, be it from Gorbachov's Soviet Union or from Latin America or from India and other third world countries. In other words, it is not just finance from the advanced capitalist flowing everywhere, largely in the form of 'hot money', for quick and speculative gains, but finance all over the globe looking for opportunities all over the globe' (Patnaik, 2003: 20). In addition to these factors, sixth implication can also be added which is in fact the culmination of all, i.e. the accumulation process. David Harvey calls it 'accumulation through dispossession'[3] (Harvey, 2003: 137-182) and for Prabhat Patnaik, it is the 'accumulation through encroachment' [4] (Patnaik, 2005).

Revivification to Assertion of Participation and Realisation of being Participants

Assertion of participation and realisation of being participants form the core of dalit movement. 'Behind all of Ambedkar's seeming separatism, separate political parties for the backward classes, special reservation of seats in political assembles and in government jobs, there was a strong, unwavering belief in the power of democratic institutions to bring about social equality. India's case might demand special techniques not found in the west, but Ambedkar's basic faith was in representative political bodies...' (Zelliot, 1996: 115). 'To empower both the [d]alits and non-[d]alits economically, he proposed that the [s]tate should be given political power for the regulation and control of both key industries and agriculture. To this end, he proposed the economic powers should be incorporated into the body of the constitution itself' (Guru, 2000: 97).

Indian State in the post-colonial period has assumed a role of an interventionist one to bring about social transformation. It aims at eradicating feudal hierarchical social order based on Brahmanical ideology and building an egalitarian secular modern society guided by liberal values. In the preamble to the Indian Constitution, it is solemnly resolved to provide all its citizens social, economic and political justice; liberty of thought and expressions, belief, faith and worship; equality of opportunity and status and fraternity assuring the dignity of the individual. These objectives are the result of the struggle of the masses not only against the foreign rule but also against an exploitative and overwhelmingly dominant feudal class (Shah, 2002: 15).

The [s]tate has intervened in favour of [d]alits in different ways. These include: an array of constitutional and legal provisions, positive discrimination in government employment as well as in elected representative bodies through reservations, budgetary support through the special component plan (SCP) approach, special programmes for health and education; priority to SCs in all rural development, slum improvement and anti-poverty programmes, and technological changes such as conversion of dry latrines to flush latrines, for the release of persons engaged in traditional occupations (Mander, 2002: 157). In other words, the participation and realisation of being participants connote the issue of partaking in decision making process, accountability of the representative vis-à-vis people, protection and assertion for the pursuance of a dignified life via the Constitution viz. Articles 15, 16, 38, 46, 164, 275, 330, 332, 334, 335, 338, 340, 341, 342 and 366.

The most significant aspect of participation and realisation of being participants is to ensure the nullification of caste/untouchability and rendering economic rights. Therefore, in respect of untouchability and caste oppression, there has been reservation in the Legislature. The defining aspect of reservation in terms of representation in the Legislature is to ensure the sensibility, apposite intervention and initiation of measures to transform the social and economic structures. The following acts are the finest example of sensibility, intervention and initiation: The prevention of Civil Rights Act (1955), the Bonded Labour System (Abolition) Act (1976), the Minimum Wages Act (1984), the Child Labour (Prohibition and Regulation) Act (1986) and The Scheduled Castes and Scheduled Tribes (Prevention of Atrocities) Act (1989).

Concerning economic rights and its vitality, Ambedkar appositely calls attention.

> What we must do is not be content with mere political democracy. We must make our political democracy a social democracy as well. Political democracy cannot last unless there lies at the base of it a social democracy...We must begin by acknowledging the fact that there is complete absence of two things in Indian society. One of these is equality. On the social plane, we have in India a society based on the principle of graded inequality, which means elevation for some and degradation for others. On the economic plane, we have a society in which there are some who have immense wealth as against many who live in abject poverty (Ambedkar, 1986: 39-40).

His forewarning was that

> On 26th January 1950, we are going to enter into a life of contradictions. In politics, we will have equality and in social and economic structure, continue to deny the principle of one man one value. How long shall we continue to live this life of contradictions? How long shall we continue to deny equality in our social and economic life? If we continue to deny it for

> long, we will do so only by putting our political democracy in peril. We must remove this contradiction at the earliest possible moment else those who suffer from inequality will blow up the structure of democracy, which this Constituent Assembly has so laboriously built up (Ambedkar, 1986: 39-40).

Therefore, the task of the participation and realisation of being participants has been the best defence of the necessity principle. The participation and realisation of being participants espouse the non-negotiability of two aspects: employment and welfare measures. The necessity principle adheres to the position that primary responsibility, *inter alia*, of the government is to provide jobs to dalits via affirmative action. And the second aspect is the investment in the realms of education, health, house, water and so on. Both aspects constitute empowerment and envisage the subjugation-free world, resulting in non-negotiable variables. The fundamental aspect of participation and realisation of being participants has to ensure the availability of these as non-negotiable resources. The non-negotiability of resources, according to Ambedkar, is the fulcrum to obliterate the economic exploitation.[5]

Invalidation of Participation and Realisation of being Participants and its Resultant Consequences

The execution of participation and realisation of being participants, through sensibility, intervention and initiation, has to be in consonance with the people's struggles. In general, the Legislatures and the people establish a dialectical relationship with each other. The former becomes accountable to the struggling people. Thereby, representation of dalits in the Legislature does mean the initiation along with accountability of the representatives in terms of social reconstruction. This one has been a significant right enshrined in the Constitution. The right to vote, participation and accountability of the representatives pave the way for the assertion of dalits and others. The assertion promises to lead a dignified life while dethroning brahmanical and casteist imbroglio. Assertion is the feeling of belongingness to the present and the motivational factor to shape the future. Assertion is also contingent on safeguarding the spirit and functionality of participation and realisation of being participants.

In this backdrop, functionality of globalisation becomes crucial. The functionality of globalisation contravenes the participation and realisation of being participants. The participation and realisation of being participants not only ensure the dalits' partaking in decision-making process but also ensure the exhibition of acme-sensibility, intervention and initiation by the legislators and legislatures. Owing to this, independent functioning becomes crucial. The government which adopts globalisation certainly cannot function independently. Both make an oxymoron. Either of the two, government or globalisation, can function independently; both cannot go in concert. The reason is that the envisioning of the global cannot be complete without complete withdrawal of interventionist agency that is the state. The state has been a constraint. What is the constraint? This could be the state activism; functionality aspect of the state entails the independent decision-making process by the governments elected by the people and accountability of governments to the people. In other words, the participation and realisation of being participants guarantee the government functionality in favour of the dalits due to accountability. Since the underlying fact of need principle is the withdrawal of the governmental presence, and governments are willingly accepting it, in this context, the participation and realisation of being participants become toothless. Put differently, the acceptance of globalisation (the global and doing away with all constraints) necessarily invalidates the participation and realisation of being participants due to its non-functionality.

The increased caste atrocities against dalits are the direct outcome of the invalidation of participation and realisation of being participants, be it pre-globalisation era or the present days. According to 'Reports on Crime in India', National Crime Records Bureau, Ministry of Home Affairs, Government of India, crimes against dalits have increased disproportionately. According to Sukhdeo Thorat, '[t]he official statistics for the decadal period 1990 to 2000 indicate that a total of 285,871 cases of various crimes were registered countrywide by SCs, of which 14,030 were registered under the PCR Act and 81,796 under the POA Act. This means that an average of 28,587 cases of caste discrimination and atrocities were registered by SCs every year during the 1990s. In 2001, the number of cases was higher at 33,500' (Thorat, 2009: 144-145).

In the absence of independent functioning of the government and withdrawal from activism in terms of turning these non-negotiable variables into negotiable through the market, providing jobs and welfare measures have ceased to exist (the following realms and sources reveal the condition of dalits over the years in place of improvement, has become more despicable; and the contrast between dalits and non-ST populace in the Hindus has become much wider in terms of 'Education', 'Employment, 'Rural Areas', 'Rural Non-Farm Employment', 'Average Consumer Expenditure Per Capita Per Day' (PCPD), 'Monthly Per Capita Expenditure' (MPCE), and 'Health'[6]).

The closure of the public sectors, less expenditure on social sector to maintain balance of payment and austerity as enforced by IMF, and abnegation of any responsibility on the part of the market has made the economic rights given by the Constitution and achieved through struggle invalid. Under the influence of the need principle, the minimum bare availability of life-supporting variables have been shifted to the market whereby the negotiator's ability would decide the availability of resources.

Defence of Globalisation and the Issue of Four 'Veiled' Concerns

Defenders of globalisation for dalits falter on four grounds. They do not pay sufficient and required attention to the consequence of globalisation, reconstruction of the being, comparison between dalit capital and black capital and the Bhopal Declaration (Bhopal Declaration is significantly different from the Bhopal Document). This section discusses all of these four.

Ignoring the Consequence

Intriguingly and bafflingly, the defenders of globalisation for dalits adopt two pronged strategies. The first strategy reveals that the defenders of globalisation for dalits certainly share the need principle through which globalisation has been accentuated. They certainly stand for the envisioning of the global and do away with the constraints formulae—these two are the driving force of globalisation. In other words, there has been an acceptance of theoretical postulation of globalisation. The second strategy is the adoption of ominous silence vis-à-vis the outcome of the theoretical postulation of globalisation.

In a way, they adopt disjunctive methods. They categorically separate the celebration of 'the global' and 'do away with the constraints' from its effect on everyday life of dalits. The increased atrocities on dalits and massive pauperisation do not find space. These 'incidents' are merely treated as 'normal' to which dalits have been subjected since time immemorial. There has been no attempt to discover the nexus between the Hindutva forces and global capital. The truth is, globalisation has strengthened the already powerful brahmanical and casteist forces. The process of globalisation has catapulted the Hindutva forces several times to the Central government seat. The much celebrated Indian state by globalisation, Gujarat does two things: It keeps the incessant flow of international capital / finance intact while ensuring the continuance and implementation of the Hindutva in the state government.

Put differently, on the one hand, globalisation has goaded the pauperisation of dalits more than any other social groups since 1991. On the other hand, Hindutva has issued a slew of atrocious structural subjugations. Globalisation and Hindutva complement each other and their obvious enemies are the poor and the dalits, as has been revealed by none other than the governmental documents; strategically ignored by the defenders of globalisation for dalits.

Abandoning the Issue of Reconstruction

More than the ignorance of the outcome of globalisation, there is an attempt of complete subsidisation and omission of dalit movements' tenets by the defender of globalisation for dalits. The attempt to the subsidisation of dalits movements is reflected in terms of relegating it to mere sharing the pie in globalisation in the form of 'dalit capital' in place of combating it. The omission of tenets of globalisation is more of a grotesque attempt. Dalit movements never fought for the co-optation. Dalit movement is all about social reconstruction.

The social reconstruction is not at all mere sharing the pie. The social reconstruction vouches for the establishment of the egalitarian order. One of the important aspects of the social reconstruction is to ensure the functionality of the participation and realisation of being participants. The functionality of two (participation and realisation of being participants) goads the movement for social reconstruction. These two ensure the economic rights on the one hand and stepping up the measures to combat the caste and untouchability practices on the other hand. In concert, they all constitute inseparable entities.

The attack on both, which is making the governmental autonomy and functioning irrelevant and lesser, is an attack on the social reconstruction. These two are hard achieved by massive struggle. Therefore, the attack on both is the massive onslaught on the struggle for the social reconstruction and its achievements. The bypassing of the issue of social reconstruction by the defender of the globalisation for dalits is a deliberate move. The omission of the social reconstruction per se is equal to the dropping of the participation and realisation of being participants.

The omission of social reconstruction helps the defender not to engage with the issue of participation and realisation of being participants which has been the worst sufferer of globalisation. In other words, non-engagement with these two leads to non-explication between the participation and realisation of being participants and globalisation and the way the latter impacts the former. Therefore, explanation concerning the negativity of globalisation on participation and realisation of being participants and social reconstruction has been evaded by the defenders through omitting it.

Dalit Capital and Black Capital

Milind Kamble, Chairman of Dalit Indian Chamber of Commerce & Industry (DICCI), suggests that '[t]he way Black Capitalism galvanized the African Americans in America, our Dalit Capitalism ought to play a similar role back home'[7]. While analysing the issue of dalit capitalist and black capitalist, there has also been the omission of 'the participation and realisation of being participants' axiom. Since the Revolution in 1776 in the United States of America, the American society has witnessed the struggle for the civil rights. The massive struggle like 'the National Association for the Advancement of Colored People' (NAACP) (1909) and 'Selma To Montgomery Marches' (1965) culminated into Civil Rights Act of 1964 (Proscribing Racial Segregation) and the Voting Rights Act of 1965 (Proscribing discriminatory voting practices). The recognition of these rights became landmarks for the African Americans to assert their participation and realisation of being participants.

As the movement changed from a Civil Rights one to an anti-poverty one, the Nixon administration engineered the theory of Black Capitalism. A few years before the emergence of this term, an Ambedkar of the Black liberation movement, Dr. W.E.B. Du Bois, pointed out that a theory of Black Capitalism 'will insert into the ranks of the Negro race a new cause of division, a new attempt to subject the masses of the race to an exploiting capitalist class of their own people'. This is exactly what has occurred, and we now have this situation: the median income of African Americans is 66% that of whites, whereas the net worth of African Americans is only 15% that of whites (in the two top income brackets, African-Americans hold only about a third of the wealth of whites). It should also be pointed out that there are more African Americans in prison than ever before, indeed that there are more African American men in prison than in college (Prashad, 2005).

The President of the National Association for the Advancement of Colored People, Julian Bond, laid out the problems of today in his July 2005 speech, 'One central issue on the civil rights agenda—economic justice—remains unfulfilled and largely unaddressed. That there are more black millionaires today is a tribute to the movement King led. That there are proportionately fewer blacks working today is an indictment of our times and our economic system, a reflection of our challenges in keeping the movement coming on' (cited in Prashad, 2005).

The emergence of Black Capitalism has proved to be hardly of any use for African Americans in terms of employment or ending discrimination. This would be applicable for dalits also. However, the issue of participation and realisation of being participants seems more pertinent. Like African Americans, dalit movement has struggled hard to ensure the functionality of participation and realisation of being participants. The truth is that these rights became significant during pre-globalisation era in terms of lessening the caste atrocities and economic alleviation. Though the desired results were never achieved, the struggle to achieve these continues. In place of intensification of struggle, the defenders of globalisation for dalits seek the adoption of globalisation which means the surrender of struggle concerning implementation of participation and realisation of being participants. As we have seen, the curtailment of participation and realisation of being participants has led to the intensification of caste atrocities and pauperisation of dalits. The abandoning of the struggle for the participation and realisation of being participants, which is much needed for social reconstruction while ensuring economic rights, is abnegating the issue of social reconstruction. Even in the case of African Americans, despite the implementation of participation and realisation of being participants and production of black capitalism, the discrimination has grown manifold. Therefore what is needed in place of globalisation or dalit capitalism which seeks the surrender of the struggle against globalisation concerning social reconstruction, is the intensification of the struggle for the reclamation of participation and realisation of being participants, which is an intrinsic aspect of the dalit movement.

Contradicting the Bhopal Declaration

The Bhopal Declaration, adopted unanimously by the Bhopal Conference, charting a new course for dalits for the 21st century held at Bhopal, Madhya Pradesh, India, 12–13 January (2002) primarily contradicts not only the Bhopal Document (according to page number ii, 'the Government of Madhya Pradesh has prepared the Bhopal Document. The dalit Agenda was drafted by Chandra Bhan Prasad.' 'The Bhopal Document is being circulated to select individuals in advance of the Bhopal conference, January 12-13, 2002') but also myriad postulations in defence of globalisation. Put differently, the Bhopal Declaration emphasises on 21-point action agenda for the 21st century.

The declaration is an absolute assertion of participation and realisation of being participants for the implementation of economic rights while fighting the caste atrocities. There are twenty-one points and almost all points envisage the role of the government in ensuring the economic rights and protection in the cases of caste atrocities. The following are the spheres, wherein the government's role concerning the dalits is needed or sought by the declaration: 'cultivable land (point one), rural and urban common property resources (point two), dalit agricultural labourers (point three), concerning all the dalit lands occupied by non-dalits (point four), alienated lands to the tribals (point five), democratise capital (point six), the Bonded Labour System (Abolition) Act, 1976 (point seven), amendment of Art. 21 of the Constitution of India so as to include the various rights (point eight), education (point nine), reservation in the public and private educational institutions (point ten), SC and ST women as a distinct category (point eleven), implement effectively in letter and spirit the SC and ST (Prevention of Atrocities) Act, 1989 & Rules, 1995 (point twelve), diversity in all public institutions of India (point thirteen), all state and national budgets allocations (point fourteen), supplier diversity (point fifteen), sole responsibility of the state in protecting dalits (point sixteen), elimination of humiliating practices (point seventeen), annual debate by the Legislature (point nineteen), affirmative actions in all private institutions qua government institutions (point nineteen), reservation in judiciary and defence forces (point twenty) and mandatory truth chapter in two years on the status of reservation' (point twenty one).

In other words, the Bhopal Declaration is not only a revolutionary intervention but one of the best defences of the social reconstruction. The various points highlight the need of the government to deal with the atrocities issues and economic rights. Some of the participants of the Bhopal Conference, of which the Bhopal Declaration is the outcome, ironically eulogise globalisation as a great emancipator. The defence of globalisation for dalits is a nullification of the governmental responsibility. Put it differently, defence of globalisation and necessity of the government cannot go in concert. The position taken by the defenders of globalisation is, in other words, the rejection of the Declaration.

The last twenty two years, since the adoption of globalisation, suggested by none other than the various governmental committees and commissions, have witnessed more miserable condition of India and especially of dalits in terms of atrocities and pauperisation. The triumph of globalisation is the rout of the participation and realisation of being participants. Moreover, adherence to the declaration in terms of acceptance is the negation of globalisation and its defenders and avowal of participation and realisation of being participants, much needed for the social reconstruction. Therefore, the progressive forces of this country have to struggle to materialise the declaration which means nothing but the obliteration of Brahmanism and globalisation and the nexus of both.

NOTES

1. Later, Gail Omvedt takes an altogether different position by referring globalisation as 'Brahmanic Globalisation' (Omvedt, 2011: 67-73). 'By the 1990s, dalits and OBCs– "other backward castes", the new name for the ex-shudras, deriving from the Mandal commission-were organising in new ways, representing a challenge to Hindutva, brahmanic globalisation and social-economic inequalities' (Omvedt, 2011: 73).
2. Adam Smith's case is more complex because the idea of division of labour resulting in dexterity and unintended work which promotes societal goods should be considered as important contributions. His emphasis remains important:

   By preferring the support of domestic to that of foreign industry, he intends only his own security; and by directing that industry in such a manner as its produce may be the of the greatest value, he intends only his own gain, and he is in this, as in many other cases, led by an invisible hand to promote an end which was no part of his intention. Nor is it always the worst for the society that it was no part of it. By pursuing his own interest, he frequently promotes that of the society more effectually than when he really intends to promote it (Smith, 2003: 572).

3. David Harvey makes it easy to understand.

   Consider, for example, a process in US housing markets known as 'flipping'. A house in poor condition is bought for next to nothing, given some cosmetic improvements, and then sold on at an exorbitant price, with the aid of a mortgage package arranged by the seller, to a low-income family looking to realize its dream of home ownership. If the family has difficulty meeting the payments or dealing with the serious maintenance problems that almost certainly emerge, then the house is repossessed. This is not exactly illegal (buyers beware!) but the effect is to prey upon low-income families and milk them of whatever little savings they have. This is accumulation by dispossession. There are innumerable activities (legal and illegal) of this kind that affect the control of assets by one class rather than another (Harvey, 2003: 152-153).

4. Patnaik explicates that

   This burgeoning of "accumulation through encroachment" is in turn the direct result of the pursuit of "neo-liberal" policies. "Neo-liberalism" operates in this respect in two distinct ways. The first way... is the pursuit of policies that remove restrictions on the movement of goods and capital across borders. "Trade liberalization" ousts small domestic producers from the market and generally engenders domestic "de-industrialization" (in the sense of increasing unemployment through shrinking domestic industrial activity); and liberalization of capital flows allows MNCs to buy up domestic producers through a combination of carrot-and-stick methods. The second way is through the imposition of "deflationary policies", especially on government expenditure, as part of the neo-liberal agenda. This...leads to centralization of capital on a global scale, a shift in the terms of trade against the peasantry and third world primary commodity producers who become easy preys for expropriation, and a rolling back of the State sector which becomes increasingly privatized and whose domain gets opened up as a province of private accumulation) (Patnaik, 2005).

5. According to him,
   The United States of India shall declare as a part of the law of its constitution (1) That industries which are key industries or which may be declared to be key industries shall be owned and run by the State; (2) That industries which are not key industries but which are basic industries shall be owned by the State and shall be run by the State or by Corporations established by the State; (3) That Insurance shall be a monopoly of the State and that the State shall compel every adult citizen to take out a life insurance policy commensurate with his wages as may be prescribed by the Legislature; (4) That agriculture shall be State Industry; (5) That State shall acquire the subsisting rights in such industries, insurance and agricultural land held by private individuals, whether as owners, tenants or mortgagees and pay them compensation in the form of debenture equal to the value of his or her right in the land provided that in reckoning the value of land, plant or security no account shall be taken of any rise therein due to emergency, of any potential or unearned value or any value for compulsory acquisition; (6) The State shall determine how and when the debenture holder shall be entitled to claim cash payment; (7) The debenture shall be transferable and inheritable property but neither the debenture holder nor the transferee from the original holder nor his heir shall be entitled to claim the return of the land or interest in any industrial concern acquired by the State or be entitled to deal with it in any way; (8) The debenture holder shall be entitled to interest on his debenture at such rate as may be defined by law, to be paid by the State in cash or in kind as the State may deem fit; (9) Agricultural industry shall be organized on the following basis: (i) The State shall divide the land acquired into farms of standard size and let out the farms for cultivation to residents of the village as tenants (made up of group of families) to cultivate on the following conditions: (a)The farm shall be cultivated as a collective farm; (b)The farm shall be cultivated in accordance with rules and directions issued by Government; (c) The tenants shall share among themselves

in the manner prescribed the produce of the farm left after the payment of charges properly leviable on the farm; (ii) The land shall be let out to villagers without distinction of caste or creed and in such manner that there will be no landlord, no tenant and no landless labourer ; (iii) It shall be the obligation of the State to finance the cultivation of the collective farms by the supply of water, draft animals, implements, manure, seeds, etc.; (iv) The State shall be entitled to (a) levy the following charges on the produce of the farm: a portion for land revenue; a portion to pay the debenture-holders ; and (i) a portion to pay for the use of capital goods supplied; and (ii) to prescribe penalties against tenants who break the conditions of tenancy or wilfully neglect to make the best use of the means of cultivation offered by the State or otherwise act prejudicially to the scheme of collective farming; and (10) The scheme shall be brought into operation as early as possible but in no case shall the period extend beyond the tenth year from the date of the Constitution coming into operation (Ambedkar, 1979: 396-397).

6. On education, sources are: Education Statics at a glance 2005–06, Government of India, Ministry of Human Resource Development, Department of Education (2008); EFA Global Monitoring Report (2008) UNESCO; Global Education Digest (2007) UNESCO; Report on Literacy Rate, Planning Commission; NSSO 61st Round Schedule 10, 2004–2005; Time Series Data, Department of Higher Education, Ministry of Human Resource Development, Government of India.

   For employment status, references are: Various Reports of Planning Commission, CSO, and NSSO, Government of India; Eleventh Plan Document /Economic Survey 2007–08, Government of India; Directorate General of Employment & Training, Government of India; Public Enterprises Survey, Annual Report, Ministry of Heavy Industries and Public Enterprises (Various Years), Annual Reports, Ministry of Personnel, Public Grievances and Pensions (Various Years); Annual Reports (Various Years), Ministry of Finance, Government of India.

   Condition of rural areas can be fathomed through Agricultural Census (various years till 2000–01), Department of Agriculture & Co-operation, Ministry of Agriculture,

Government of India; NSS Report No. 491, 492 and 493, 2003.

Rural Non-Farm Employment is being exhibited in Special Report on Employment, Unemployment for the Social Groups, National Sample Survey (various years).

For 'Average Consumer Expenditure Per Capita Per Day' (PCPD), powerful reference is Arjun Sengupta Committee (2007), Report on Conditions of Work and Promotion of Livelihoods in the Organised Sector, National Commission for Enterprises in the Unorganised Sector, Government of India.

'Monthly Per Capita Expenditure' (MPCE) has been highlighted in Sachar Committee Report (2006), Social, Economic and Educational Status of the Muslim Community of India, Prime Minister's High Level Committee, Cabinet Secretariat, Government of India.

Health's references are: World Health Report 2003 and 2008; UNDP Human Development Report 2003; Report on Currency and Finance (various issues), Reserve Bank of India; Statistical Abstract of India, (various issues) Government of India; Handbook of Statistics of India, (various issue) Reserve Bank of India; Economic Survey 2007–08; Planning Commission, Ministry of Health and Family Welfare; 2005–2006, National Family Health Survey(NFHS-3), National Fact Sheet INDIA(Provisional Data), Ministry of Health and family Welfare, Government of India; Key Indicators from NFHS-3(2005–06) by Wealth Index and Caste/Tribe, India (Provisional Data).

7. Available at http://www.dicci.org/readmore.html.

5

Foundational Knowledge and De-decentring Tendency

Education was monopolized by a class of people who were more or less 'drones in the hive, gorging at a feast to which they [had] contributed nothing'.

—B.R. Ambedkar (Ambedkar, 1990c: 6)

The struggle for people's democracy is also the struggle for the liberation of knowledge from the clutches of few. Knowledge is immensely one of the supreme values towards achieving the condition of equal beings. This chapter focuses on the relationship between foundational knowledge and de-decentring tendency and thereafter interrogates both in the context of avowal of market-led suzerainty in India. Throughout the chapter, the foundational knowledge denotes the realm of higher education. The de-decentring tendency can be construed as centralisation or centralised tendency and its return—centralisation of foundational knowledge in terms of appropriation and monopolisation. The justification of using de-decentring tendency in place of centralised tendency is based on the following premises: centralised tendency exhibits the concentration of foundational knowledge in a few hands whereas de-decentring tendency demonstrates not just this concentration but also the return of concentration in contemporary time after limited rupture.

The perusal in this chapter starts with this premise that foundational knowledge constitutes a *sine qua non* of transformative voyage. The transformation of corporeal reality through foundational knowledge and creation of corporeal reality to produce required foundational knowledge have been an incessant concern for struggling people. In a way, foundational knowledge becomes a symbol not only of protest but also of the alternative vision. The foundational knowledge *per se* denotes herein a special value —a value, which has multifaceted purposes ranging from the betterment of everyday life, to the creation of an emancipatory world, to contesting the dominant knowledge. The foundational knowledge thereby becomes an immensely significant attribute. The creation of knowledge through higher education and its copious capacity to create vital knowledge catapults higher education to influential pedestal.

Foundational and Functional Knowledge and De-decentring Tendency

The utility of higher education (hereafter foundational knowledge) has an omniscient value. It is because of this virtue, foundational knowledge does not cease to exist as an innocent sphere. The contestation over value, therefore, has had its own significance since ages. Foundational knowledge acquires an eminent space due to two pronged activities: acquisition and dissemination. The acquiring activities entail the primary responsibility of foundational knowledge that is acquiring investigatory aspects through analysis. It has three realms: epochal analysis, contemporaneous analysis and visionary certitude. In epochal analysis, odyssey of human activities in socio-political and economic spheres and applied activities like science and technology are investigated and analysed. The epochal analysis explains functionality of human activities and applied activities in the sense of genesis, ownership, utility and discrimination. The aim of contemporaneous analysis is to locate human and applied activities in terms of comprehending continuation, modification and issue of relevance of the past. Visionary certitude is one of the fulcrums of foundational knowledge and has double roles. The first role is to envisage necessarily a bettering future. The second is preparedness in case of prognosis of a miserable condition. In other words, betterment and countering eventualities are twin aspects of visionary certitude. Understandably, prevalent corporeal realities decide the nature of visionary certitude.

Considering disseminative role, the utility of foundational knowledge becomes immensely vital. On the one hand, dissemination becomes fructuous in terms of acquainting people to epochal analysis, contemporaneous analysis and visionary certitude; on the other hand, it can also obfuscate dissemination and lead to centralised tendency (hereafter de-decentring tendency). The former represents decentralised tendency whereby people could access, be empowered and utilise the foundational knowledge. The latter symbolises de-decentring tendency through which dominant forces have monopolised and obfuscated the dissemination of 'acquiring' aspect of foundational knowledge.

The de-decentring tendency has appropriated all the three aspects (epochal analysis, contemporaneous analysis and visionary certitude) in a few hands. This can be elucidated by contrasting functional knowledge and foundational knowledge. The functional knowledge is a repository of elementary *knowledges*. The functional knowledge, also known as elementary knowledge, is all about acquainting and equipping people with basic information. Equipping people with basic information is not at all a worrisome aspect for the ruling echelon. In fact, emphasis on functional knowledge has strengthened the continuation of ruling echelons in two ways: first, functional knowledge has been forcibly made the *only* component required for livelihood. Therefore, the responsibility of ruling echelons gets over with the opening of the functional knowledge institutions; second, the emphasis on 'what' is more important than 'why' in functional knowledge. Put differently, the issue of epistemology and ontology is bypassed and 'description' occupies the dominant space. Foundational knowledge is all about epistemological and ontological enterprise. In functional knowledge, these two important concerns are deliberately omitted.

Historicity of De-decentring Tendency

The contestation over foundational knowledge and its monopolisation since time immemorial have been a concern writ large for ruling echelons. Historicity of de-decentring tendency exhibits this aspect profoundly. The first phase of de-decentring tendency began with surplus accumulation and advancement in material sphere. The advancement in material sphere led to two types of development. The first development led to justification of knowledge through foundational knowledge for few classes. So they could enable the rule over property less people. This reflection is easily identifiable in Plato (Plato, 1970 & 2003) and Aristotle (Barnes, 1991a & 1991b). 'Public education was almost nonexistence in the world of Plato and Aristotle...' (Curren, 2007: 8).

'When we use or commend the upbringing of individual people', according to Plato, 'and say that one of us is educated and the other uneducated, we sometimes use this latter term for men who have, in fact, had a thorough education - one directed towards petty trade or the merchant-shipping business, or something like that. But for the purpose of the present discussion, we are not going to treat this sort of thing as "education"; what we have in mind in education from childhood in *virtue*, a training which produces a keen desire to become a perfect citizen who knows how to rule and be ruled as justice demand' (Plato, 1970: 73). Therefore, in schema of foundational knowledge, what he calls *virtue*, 'concerns itself primarily with developing the upper classes of society: the leaders and the military. For those who devote themselves to the trades and crafts and to industrial and agricultural labour: in a word, for the vast majority of the population, Plato does nothing. His system is thus, not for the many but for the few...' (Lodge and Solomon, 2000: 249).

Continuation of analogous method remained an intrinsic aspect of Aristotle. His discussion about education cannot be insulated from the state, leisure, citizenship and slavery (Aristotle, 1984). For Aristotle, education 'aims at producing such a character as will issue in acts tending to promote the happiness of the state; in the second place, it aims at preparing the soul for that right enjoyment of leisure which becomes possible when practical needs have been satisfied' (Burnet, 1980: 1). 'Since, the end of individuals and of states is the same, the end of the best man and if the best constitution must also be same; it is therefore evident that there ought to exist in both of them the excellences of leisure...' (Aristotle, 1991: 159). Consequently, he focuses on public education by the state: the public education for the citizenry. The citizenry was a propertied class and in his schema of public education to strengthen the state and common pursuit of leisure was made unavailable for non-citizenry like women, slave and outsiders. The exclusivist nature of foundational knowledge and its creation were the hallmark of this period, which get reflected categorically in Plato and Aristotle. Interestingly, in both and general character of this period, there was almost no hesitancy in terms of providing functional knowledge but foundational knowledge was out of reach for the people.

The Second development in the first phase was deprivation of education not only on class basis but also through creation of ascriptive identities. Ascriptive identity became the fulcrum to debar the access to knowledge and holding sway over the other. Dalits and others are apt examples in this regard. The irony was that the functional knowledge was allowed then to remain to exploit labour, but foundational knowledge was strictly circumvented. Various strictures and sermons are abounded in religious texts and severe punishments were envisaged and implemented. The mythological killings in various religious texts are telling aspects and have been followed verbatim. In addition, any possibility to acquire such knowledge, which could possibly destroy the class-caste duo discrimination, was botched. The example of calendar is very apt herein.

> ...brahminism must have had some peculiar function in the early means of production, sane outstanding success which gave it a grip upon society. Mere superstition cannot arise, unless it has some deep productive roots, though it may survive by inertia. One of these functions was a good calendar. It does not suffice here, as in Europe, for the agriculturist to note the end of winter by natural signs. The word for 'rain' varsa also means 'year', so important is the annual monsoon for India. The Indian farmer has to prepare his land before the monsoon sets in. The sowing can only be done after the proper rainy season begun, or the sprouts will die. The fields are best weeded during the mid-monsoon break. If the harvest be brought in before the last seasonal rain, there is every chance that grain will rot on the threshing floor. Empirical observation says that the four-month rains set in, break, and cease at approximately fixed times of the year. The real difficulty lay in telling the time of the year accurately (Kosambi, 1996: 250).

From ancient to medieval period, controlling higher education viz. creation of foundational knowledge was a process writ large. The monopolisation of foundational knowledge was absolute. This process was the reflection of the greatest misery meted out to deprived sections. In fact, in medieval period of Europe, any position challenging orthodoxy of the church in the sphere of human activities:

social-political-economic and applied activities like science-technology (whether the universe is heliocentric or geocentric), led to silencing of voices through excommunication, declaration as heretic and even awarding death penalty. In India, for deprived section despite ruling classes' interchangeability, condition remained similar. '... [T]he political structure was sustained by the *zamindars*, caste again was important, since the *zamindars*, by and large, belonged to the "dominant castes" which maintained their position by force' (Habib, 2000: 176).

The rupture with this phase became imminent due to the advent of modernity in many ways and led to the second phase. The changes that were unfolding have been categorically encapsulated by Marx and Engels in *The Communist Manifesto*:

> The bourgeoisie cannot exist without constantly revolutionising the instruments of production, and thereby the relations of production, and with them the whole relations of society. Conservation of the old modes of production in unaltered form, was, on the contrary, the first condition of existence for all earlier industrial classes. Constant revolutionising of production, uninterrupted disturbance of all social conditions, everlasting uncertainty and agitation distinguish the bourgeois epoch from all earlier ones. All fixed, fast-frozen relations, with their train of ancient and venerable prejudices and opinions, are swept away, all new-formed ones become antiquated before they can ossify. All that is solid melts into air, all that is holy is profaned, and man is at last compelled to face with sober senses his real conditions of life, and his relations with his kind (Marx and Engels, 1999: 92).

The changes in corporeal spheres were so profound that they led to hesitant responses from John Locke, Jean Jacques Rousseau and J.S. Mill. Hesitant responses mean concession to certain extent but not beyond that. One example would suffice here. Immanuel Kant is known for his 'categorical-imperative' formulation. The categorical imperative implies the '[a]ct only according to that maxim whereby you can at the same time will that it should become a universal law' (Kant, 1994: 30). One should not practice the act that cannot be replicated onto him/her. In other words, individual's body remains fulcrum of action. Despite this, he could not resist to make such remark: '...in short, this fellow [a carpenter] was quite black from head to foot, a clear proof that what he said was stupid' (Eze, 2001: 57). Similarly, John Locke suggests, '[k]nowledge and science in general is the business only of those who are at ease and leisure. Those who have particular callings ought to understand them; and it is no unreasonable proposal, nor impossible to be compassed, that they should think and reason right about what is their daily employment' (Locke, 1996: 182). Hence, foundational knowledge is not available for everyone.

According to Rousseau, nature plays a central role. For him, education is meant to recover or shape a natural man. The best utility of education is to reconcile man, nature and things so that best and holistic and internal development could take place. Rousseau suggests that, '[w]e are born weak, we need strength; we are born totally unprovided, we need aid; we are born stupid, we need judgement. Everything we do not have at our birth and which we need when we are grown is given us by education. This education comes to us from nature, from men, or from things. The internal development of our faculties and our organs is the education of nature. The use that we are taught to make of this development is the education of men. And what we acquire from own experience about the objects which affect us is the education of things' (Rousseau, 1979: 37). Put differently, education in the hands of Rousseau becomes an instrument to insulate the prevalent corrupt order in place of transforming the society. The prevalent corrupt order is explicated in *the Discourse on the Origins of Inequality*. 'Man was born free, equal, self-sufficient, unprejudiced, and whole; now, at the end of history, he is in chains (ruled by other men or by laws he did not make), defined by relations of inequality (rich or poor, noble or commoner, master or slave), dependent, full of false opinions or superstitions, and divided between his inclinations and his duties. Nature made man a brute, but happy and good' (Bloom, 1979: 3).

Return of John Locke is overtly visible in J.S. Mill in respect of knowledge creation and the state help. He remains hesitant about government-led assistance and extension to educational institutions. 'An education established and controlled by the State, should only exist, if it exist at all, as one among many competing experiments, carried on for the purpose of example and stimulus, to keep the others up to a certain standard of excellence' (Mill, 2003: 167).

Many have countered the de-decentring tendency of first phase and second phase, and it paved the way for the third phase. In fact, third phase is the phase of commencement of revolutionary claim over foundational knowledge by, inter alia, Karl Marx, Jotirao Phule and B.R. Ambedkar. Karl Marx and Frederick Engels in the *Communist Manifesto* explain societal and educational relationship. 'The Communists have not invented the intervention of society in education; they do but seek to alter the character of that intervention and to rescue education from the influence of the ruling class' (Marx and Engels, 1999: 107). In a speech on General Education for General council Meetings of International Workingmen's Association 1869, Marx stated two roles: changing social circumstances to produce desired foundational knowledge and production of foundational knowledge to change the social circumstances.

> ...there was a peculiar difficulty connected with this question [on education]. On the one hand a change of social circumstances was required to establish a proper system of education, on the other hand a proper system of education was required to bring about a change of social circumstances; we must therefore commence where we were (Small, 2005: 39).

Concordant with Marx's concern, Lenin conceives of education as 'one of the component parts of the struggle we are now waging' (Tomaik, 1974: 41). 'We say that our work in the sphere of education is part of the struggle for overthrowing the bourgeoisie. We publicly declare that education divorced from life and politics is lies and hypocrisy' (Small, 2005: 159).

Aptly describing the significance of education, Lenin elaborates its significance in following words:

> The working people are thirsting for knowledge because they need it to win. Nine out of ten of the working people have realised that knowledge is a weapon in their struggle for emancipation, that their failures are due to lack of education, and that now it is up to them really to give everyone access to education. Our cause is assured because the people have themselves set about building a new, socialist Russia. They are learning from their own experience, from their failures and mistakes, and they see how indispensable education is for the victorious conclusion of their struggle (Lenin, 1978: 88).

In 1920, N.I. Bukharin and E. Preobrazhensky elaborated the *modus operandi* of the university and foundational knowledge which according to them was 'considered in the educational section of the party programme' (Bukharin and Preobrazhensky, 1969: 290). In the university 'all distinction between professors and students will have disappeared... [Recruitment of staffs will take place] to effect the necessary revolution in the teaching of the social sciences, and will be able to expel bourgeois culture from its last refuge. Furthermore, the composition of the audiences will be changed, for most of the students will be workers, and of course in this way technical science will pass into the possession of the working class. But the attendance of the workers at the universities will necessarily involve their maintenance at the cost of the State throughout the period of instruction' (Bukharin and Preobrazhensky, 1969: 290). This is a vital contribution on accessibility and universality of fundamental knowledge when emergence of 'specialised vocational schools, in which the pupil's destiny and future activity are determined in advance' (Gramsci, 2007:27), are taking place.

In India, education as a sphere of praxis whereby theoretical and practical struggle could take place is clearly visible in Jotirao Phule, Savitribai Phule and Ambedkar along with the others. In fact, Jotirao Phule and Savitribhai Phule started the first girl school in India at Pune. Ambedkar's famous normative remark is itself a telling aspect: 'educate, organize and agitate'. Ambedkar founded *Depressed Classes Education Society* (1928) and *People's Education Society* (1945). Ambedkar posits a question '[w]hy need the Shudra bother to take to education, when there is the Brahmin to whom he can go when the occasion for reading or writing arises?' (Ambedkar, 1979: 69). His straightaway answer is '... [i]nterdependence of one class on another class is inevitable. Even dependence of one class upon another may sometimes become allowable. But why make one person depend upon another in the matter of his vital needs? Education everyone must have. Means of defence everyone must have' (Ambedkar, 1979: 69). Concerning foundational knowledge, he points that '[h]igher education in India is the monopoly of Hindus and particularly of high Caste Hindus. By reason of Untouchability the Untouchables are denied the opportunity for Education' (Ambedkar, 1990b: 417-418).

To break the monopoly over higher education, his four fold suggestions are: '(1) Governments—Union and State—shall be required to assume financial responsibility...; (2) The responsibility for finding money for secondary and college education of the Scheduled Castes in India shall be upon the State Governments and the different States shall make a provision in their annual budgets for the said purpose in proportion to the population of the Scheduled Castes to the total budget of the States; (3) The responsibility for finding money for foreign education of the Scheduled Castes shall be the responsibility of the Union Government; (4) These special grants shall be without prejudice to the right of the Scheduled Castes to share in the expenditure incurred by the state government for the advancement of primary education for the people of the State' (Ambedkar, 1979: 403).

The challenge to de-decentring tendency has been not only a challenge to foundational knowledge (acquiring and disseminative) but also to the reconstruction of material and social sphere. The pursuance of foundational knowledge herein becomes the pursuance of democratic order wherein centralisation of foundational knowledge is resisted and a more harmonious, egalitarian and accessible knowledge production is envisaged. There are four aspects: dissent, struggle, construction and purposive venture. The dissenting aspect evinces uncomfortableness with prevalent form of foundational knowledge and thereby struggling against it. This aspect is complied with germination of foundational knowledge and its utility towards transformation.

Indian State, De-decentring Tendency and Market

The independence of India and circumstantial phenomena of few centuries forced the Indian state to rupture with various ancient-medieval practices. The rupture is always contingent upon the intensity of alternative forces. Wherever and whenever alternative forces became successful, rupture from the ancient-medieval practices has been sharp. Normative claim over the state by deprived sections is one of such ruptures. Despite overt exhibition of caste and class character, normative claim over the state is contested. This has dual purpose. First, claims force heterogeneous ruling echelons to respond to it; response may be for the purpose of legitimacy or outcome of inner struggle amongst ruling echelons. Second, claim is also a form of struggle to intensify mobilisation for immediate and long-lasting causes. Claim over foundational knowledge in association with the state's help must also be understood through these concerns.

The claim over foundational knowledge in India and the

Indian state response has been an outcome of insatiable normative struggle. The exclusivity of foundational knowledge and its utility are hallmarks on India's landscape. Production, consumption and the petrifying aspect of foundational knowledge sustained an era of monolithic exploitation. The political economy and sociology of ancient-medieval era demonstrate categorically the nature of production, consumption and exclusivist possession of foundational knowledge. The modern time promises certain respite. This is due to the crumbling of ancient-medieval virtue and emergence of struggle and changing nature of the base.

After Independence, struggling and alternative forces realised the significance of foundational knowledge. The pressing aspect was to force the state to venture into it. Though outcome has not been satisfactory as envisaged, nevertheless 'claim' remains an important aspect for the state to prove its legitimacy before the people. Indian state's role has been exhibited through opening of higher institutions and providing opportunity to deprived sections. As of now (June, 2012), there are 42 central universities. The pioneer agency is the University Grant Commission (UGC), which is meant for coordination, determination, maintenance of standards and release of grants. Along with it, there are fourteen other professional councils: All India Council of Technical Education (AICTE), Medical Council of India (MCI), Indian Council of Agricultural Research (ICAR), National Council for Teacher Education (NCTE), Dental Council of India (DCI), Pharmacy Council of India (PCI), Indian Nursing Council (INC), Bar Council of India (BCI), Central Council of Homeopathy (CCH), Central Council for Indian Medicine (CCIM), Council of Architecture (CA), Distance Education Council (DEC), Council of Scientific & Industrial Research (CSIR) and Rehabilitation Council of India (RCI). These professional councils are responsible for the recognition of courses, promotion of professional institutions and provision of grants and various awards to undergraduate programmes. According to constitutional provision, education is entry number 66 in the concurrent list. It provides exclusive legislative power to the Centre in terms of overarching role over these institutions. The role of the state governments is also important. They account for 298 state universities. The state governments are responsible for initiation of state universities, colleges, state council of higher education and grants.

Put differently, these institutions are product of a 'claim' by the struggling people. It does not mean that they are perfectly working in tune with the philosophy of 'claim' for foundational knowledge. In fact, eulogisation should be desisted. Nonetheless, outcome in the form of universities and institutions for foundational knowledge and materialisation of its twin objectives (acquisition and dissemination) cannot be dismissed or negated squarely. One must remember the context. The Indian context has always been detrimental and discriminatory, based on class–caste–patriarchal tenets concerning foundational knowledge. Therefore, this was no lesser achievement albeit an unsatisfactory one.

A fortiori, mission for the foundational knowledge, has been abortive. This could have been taken further. The further jolt for this came from the acceptance and implementation of neo-liberal project. Explicitly, this is an assault on the claim. Considering claim, the opportunity of acquiring and disseminating foundational knowledge has been weakening due to market-led suzerainty. Marked-led suzerainty contravenes 'the claim principle'. Market-led suzerainty promotes asymmetrical relation resulting in de-decentring tendency once again.

After contravening the claim principle, market-led suzerainty harps on two-pronged strategy, which is visible in India: appropriation and monopolisation of foundational knowledge by the state. Both strategies have led to the accumulation and pauperisation simultaneously in respect of foundational knowledge. Appropriation of state led foundational knowledge and thereafter its monopolisation is visible in the sphere of science and applied sciences. The recent tendency clearly points out four trends in India: (a) individualised research in the sphere of sciences; (b) commoditisation of research; (c) surplus accumulation and (d) 'distanciation' of the fruits of research. The individualised research in sciences has been promoted at the cost of collectivity. Individual based project, association and collaboration with private capital in the camouflaged name of public–private partnership (PPP) has produced a particular kind of research. The identification and exploration have been dictated under the terms of PPP and patent nomenclature. For individuals, identification of problem rests on the viability of patent and sponsorship. The most desired areas wherein research could take place are bypassed. The outcome of research gets commodified, enhancing the private partnership and individuals located in the state-run institutions. This, of course, leads to accumulation on the basis of foundational knowledge. Consequently, the fruits of research are withheld from reaching the people.

Put more precisely, four areas could be identified wherein appropriation of foundational knowledge has taken place through campus selection, partnership and investment. They are 'Technology', 'Medical Services', 'Commerce' and 'Agricultural Sphere'. The de-decentring tendency in the form of appropriation in these four spheres has strengthened the expansion of private companies and monopolisation of resources. For example, before 1991, various kinds of research in previously mentioned spheres was confined and rested with governments and utility was *principally* meant for the people. Post 1991 era has shown the new scale of appropriation and expansion of companies. The biggest beneficiaries of erstwhile and present science research are

Reliance, Tata, and Airtel in telecommunication; Wipro and Infosys in software; Fortis, Apollo, Max Health Care in medical sciences; financial conglomerates in commerce-related higher education (MBA, CA, CS, ICWA and Research) and recently in Agriculture, Monsanto and Dow.

Agriculture Institutions and Universities were earlier engaged in the development of hybrid and high-yielding varieties. To achieve this, the National Seed Corporation was set up. The Seeds Act was passed in 1966 to regulate the growing seed industry. This led to the production of various varieties and the resultant food sufficiency. The new seed policy in 1988 led to the emergence of interventionist aspect by MNCs. Now seeds are not public property but 'intellectual property' of MNCs. Monsanto, Du Pont, Mitsui, Syngenta, Aventis and Dow control 98% of the world's seed market including India as well; MNCs directly or indirectly control a major share of the seed market. These companies also have monopoly over pesticides. Now, IARI and ICAI, along with other agricultural research institutes, have collaborated with giant seed companies and are siphoning off the resources to them. The Indo–US Knowledge Initiative on Agriculture (KIA) is another justification of monopoly of Monsanto, which is also on the KIA Board. Monsanto has signed an agreement with ICAR to control Bt Brinjal (All India Kisan Sabha, 2010).

De-decentring philosophy in the sphere of social science and applied social sciences has adhered to through three ways. The first is the creation of agencies. In other words, dominant social sciences have become agencies in three forms: pedagogical masculinity, pedagogical casteism and pedagogical classism. Various researches have proved the presence of three aspects prevalent in social sciences. Social sciences despite being agencies create subject in form of particular shaping. Along with this, learners and practioners of social sciences are being perceived as laid off spheres. This creates another dimension that is the annulment of praxis.

Social sciences are deliberately made redundant to avoid praxis. For this purpose, less grant is a recurring phenomenon. Furthermore, there are two kinds of attempts: (a) construction and promotions of social scientists by insulating text from practices; and (b) endorsement of social scientists who are responding to the reality of the 'other real' and thereby negating the original real. This leads to creation of utility-based comprehension of social sciences which have the following features: 'insulation of history', 'insulation of theory', 'social sciences as administered tool: introduction of courses to suit the administering needs', 'collection of mere empirical subjects' and 'appointments of social scientists as administrative heads rather than transformative agents'.

The monopoly of foundational knowledge has been attempted vigorously. This is visible in the form of 138 private universities and foreign universities as proposed by the Foreign University Entry and Operation Bill. This has been reinforced by Punnaya Committee (UGC, 1993), Swaminathan Committee (AICTE, 1994) Birla-Ambani Report on the Policy Framework for Reforms in Education (2000) and the Foreign University Entry and Operation Bill (2010). In social sciences, the construction of particular epistemological realm has became rampant in the form of big industrialist houses led think tanks, institutes funded by agencies and prioritising their epistemological construction by the state and ruling echelons over alternative epistemologies.

In lieu of Conclusion

The best possible way to counter the de-decentring tendency is to reinvigorate the claim principle. It would, on the one side, resist the appropriation and monopolisation of foundational knowledge in the hands of ruling echelons and on the other, it could restore the claim over foundational knowledge in terms of acquisition (epochal analysis, contemporaneous analysis and visionary certitude) and dissemination. The claim for foundational knowledge is extremely vital for the transformation, especially of higher education, collectivisation of science research, promotion of social science as transformative agents through adherence to 'plurality and reality', de-caste', 'de-class' and 'de-patriarchy' values.

6

India, Pakistan and Coalescence History of People

We know only a single science, the science of history.
—Karl Marx and Frederick Engels, German Ideology
(Marx and Engels, 1976: 28)

History is principally an act of thought.
—Benedetto Croce (Croce, 1921: 19)

Toynbee has failed to see this because his general conception of history is ultimately naturalistic; he regards the life of a society as a natural and not a mental life, something at bottom merely biological and best understood on biological analogies. And this is connected with the fact that he never reaches the conception of historical knowledge as the re-enactment of the past in the historian's mind.
—R.G. Collingwood (Collingwood, 1994: 163)

If, however, these are some of the insights of what I may call the Collingwood view of history, it is time to consider some of the dangers. The emphasis on the role of the historian in the making of history tends, if pressed to its logical conclusion, to rule out any objective history at all: history is what the historian makes.
—E.H. Carr (Carr, 1987: 26)

This chapter must be understood in the context of people's democracy. Principles of foreign policies cannot be devoid of democratic practices or public scrutiny in a democracy. Nonetheless, information remains unavailable for years under the pretext of security and stability concerns. From people's democracy perspective, there are two significant violations. Firstly, foreign policies or treaties remain beyond public gaze; for example, many papers of war period in both countries are not revealed. In India, for example treaties with foreign countries are not required to be discussed in the Parliament. Secondly, in the absence of public scrutiny and debate, only the ruling elites construct foreign policy, making people unaware of certain foreign policy issues. It becomes complex in case of India and Pakistan where history paves the way for contemporaneity. Contemporaneity denotes the *only* significance of the present and immediate need as well.

Limit of Exchanged Relationship/Foreign Policy

Foreign policy encompasses multiple meanings and practices. Dominantly, it has been interpreted and practiced as 'exchanged relationship'. 'Exchanged relationship' underlines the vitality of relationship through diplomacy, commodity, people, tactical support (often occasional), military and market exchange of each other. Foreign policy as model of 'exchanged relationship' can be gauged in the theorists of international relations[1] and views and practices of career diplomat. The utility of 'exchanged relationship' can be located in the context of those countries where existence of each runs parallel against the other. Put differently, many continental countries have altogether different existence not only territorially but also ethnically. Foreign policy as 'exchanged relationship' in this context becomes a method of reconciliation of contradiction. It is like knowing an alien land, utilising relations to know the functioning of each other. Exchanged relationship can be channelised by way of high summits.

The limit of exchanged relationship is its contextual applicability. It is very difficult and highly unconvincing to apply it in those countries where history is common but territorial division was the outcome of imperialism. Here, the principal contradiction is not in being an alien land but producing of an alien land. Exchanged relationship does not go much deeper. The present chapter analyses India-Pakistan relationship from the perspective of coalescence history of people. This chapter attempts to highlight three zones wherefrom coalescence history of people is replaced by the interest of ruling echelons who hark back on an 'autonomy' of their own, by prioritising 'contested zones' and exclusively defined 'mutual terrain'[2].

Coalescence History of People

Coalescence history is a history of commons. The conflict between coalescence history and contemporaneity and priority of the latter over the former produces some phantasmagorical consequences. Especially, when contemporaneity is prioritised over history or becomes a vantage point to assess the history, it produces fixation of time and space. A particular commonality is also recognised by Sujata Bose and Ayesha Jalal. According to them,

> It is a commonplace in any introduction to South Asian history to expound on the cliché about the region's unity in diversity. It may be more appropriate to characterize South Asia and its people as presenting a picture of diversity in unity, indeed of immense diversity within a very broad contour of unity. The geographical boundaries drawn by the highest mountain ranges in the world and encircling seas and oceans set the whole of the subcontinent apart from the rest of the world. Yet within these boundaries there is great diversity in natural attributes-imposing hills and mountains, lush green river plains, arid deserts and brown plateaus. Peoples inhabiting such a clearly defined, yet diverse, region have evolved a shared cultural ambience, but at the same time are deeply attached to distinctive cultural beliefs and practices (Bose and Jalal, 2004: 3-4).

The tragedy of history in South Asia is not the arrival of unity by recourse to common history but the fragmentation of history by making contemporaneity a vantage point. South

Asian region encompasses numerous contemporaneities but one history. This history is neither unilinear nor homogeneous. South Asian history remarkably suggests that this history is a coalescence history. The definitional aspect of history is being modified by a *status quo*. History is attached unhesitatingly with both organic and inorganic elements. History is the real consequence of human progression. Here, progression entails continuum changing in real world along with thought and knowledge. Change might not occur as desired by us. Despite this, the fingerprint of history is undeniable or cannot be shrugged off casually. Coalescence history is used here as the history of the past. Nevertheless, South Asian history demands specific attention. Herein, history of events is not as important as coalescence history. Coalescence history suggests that the people of this region have intertwined in many ways. Idiosyncrasies of particularities have become universalities. Universalities have reduced particularities. Omniscient values are defined, redefined and accepted partially. Distortion of singularities is the hallmark of South Asian region. Distortion is good for intermingling but ominous as well, when ascriptive hierarchies are being spread all over along with class division.

One of the devastating impacts of colonialism was the initiation of formation of a communal identity. The formations of communal identity, on the one hand, laid down the division on the basis of religion, and on the other hand, internal contradictions were jettisoned in each religion. The difficulty with the coalescence history is that it cannot be washed away. Scaled formation of religious identity cannot take away innumerable practices imbibed and inculcated by people divided on religious lines; but division on the line of religion which is a reflection of political economy or augmentation of the means of production was made to turn into permanent division, completely bypassing the people who have been treated as an appendage in the workshop of history. Coalescence history, which suggests that we all are affected by each other massively and 'each' history is abortive without 'other', started to fade out and was omitted by the time of withdrawal of colonial masters. Now, leadership of religio-communal formations worked hard to cleanse the coalescence history without much success. However, it can be subsided by looking back at the history from contemporaneity[3]. The immediate advantage here is the *impromptu* construction of perspective which is dubbed as history. Now onwards, history is seen as required by the contemporary time. And the contemporary time is better than yesteryears in terms of production of large-scale information which provides perspective and is eventually treated as history. The tragedy of South Asia is also an intrinsic tragedy of India-Pakistan. Coalescence history of people of both countries is negated and taken over by ruling echelons for which history is nothing but contemporary interest. The next section attempts to explain the global signification of India and Pakistan.

India, Pakistan and Global Signification

Signification of India-Pakistan relationship in the global context becomes extremely noteworthy. There are four significations attached to both the countries since the independence in 1947 which have become extremely vital for global/imperialist forces. The significations are not arrived at by both countries but have been imposed preposterously. Therefore, a question of consensus does not crop up but consent becomes important. Ruling leadership of both countries does not agree on issues which are vital for both, thus outrightly negating consensuses. However, same leadership readily gives its agreement about its fate as far as imperialist masters are concerned, on the construction of meaning of both.

Firstly, 'existence' has become *fait accompli* in global discourse concerning both countries. The capitalist discourse perceives both countries' relationship as an existential question. According to Samuel Huntington,

> In the post-Cold War world, India's relations with Pakistan are likely to remain highly conflictual over Kashmir, nuclear weapons, and the overall military balance on the Subcontinent. To the extent that Pakistan is able to win support from other Muslim countries, India's relations with Islam generally will be difficult. To counter this, India is likely to make special efforts, as it has in the past, to persuade individual Muslim countries to distance themselves from Pakistan (Huntington, 1996: 244).

Agenda from policy making to research in universities/ institutions in the West has been zeroed in on existence as if other contradictions have been resolved i.e. bypassing other issues but the existence of two.

Secondly, 'strategic' preponderance remains circulating values to engage with countries. Certain words such as 'terrorism' and 'balance of power in Asia' are repeated epithets. Pakistan's importance for the Western World has been to fight terrorism and safeguard their interest. Despite the difference of opinion in European and American bourgeoisie as to whether the economy is important or ideology, there is no meaning of Pakistan for Pakistan herein. Pakistan becomes insignificant for itself and helpful for others. Stephen P. Cohen states,

> Pakistan's international supporters were ambivalent about democracy too. The American Agenda was clear: a pro-Western Pakistan, a stable Pakistan, a prosperous Pakistan, and a democratic Pakistan were all desirable, but in that order. When democracy threatened to remove a leadership that was less than pro-American, the U.S. Embassy conveyed this priority to Pakistanis and for decades got a hearing-over the years the embassy, and most ambassadors, have been major participants in the Pakistani political process, even when they did not seek such influence (Cohen, 2004: 56-57).

India's location is understood greatly in Waltzian ways i.e.

balance of power per se. According to Waltz, '[f]rom Machiavelli through Meinecke and Morgenthau the elements of the approach of and the reasoning remain constant' (Waltz, 1979: 117). Moreover, '[i]f there is any distinctly political theory of international politics, balance-of-power is it' (Waltz, 1979: 117). The role of India, in this regard, is to balance China and other economic powers of Asia. Aijaz Ahmad commented long back that '[a]side from a possible short-term irritation, the long term prospect is for a closer anti-China axis between the United States and India' (Ahmad, 2000: 241) [4].

Thirdly, Military Industry Complex (MIC) defines the signification of India-Pakistan for the expansion of arms markets. 'First identified in a speech by President Eisenhower in 1961, it had been in being from the earliest days of the confluence of American industrial capacity and international military commitment, specifically the Great War of 1914–1918. Organized at the highest level of government and industry, the Military-Industrial Complex was born of war and fed by American industry' (Pavelec, 2010: XV). Noam Chomsky suggests that '[y]ou must pretend that we're under threat of attack by Guatemala or Nicaragua if they get a MiG for self-defense against U.S. attack in order to frighten the public into accepting what's actually happening. That's the real military-industrial complex' (Chomsky, 2004).

According to Stockholm International Peace Research Institute, '[t]he four largest importers of conventional weapons in 2006–10 are located in Asia: India (9 per cent of all imports), China (6 per cent), South Korea (6 per cent) and Pakistan (5 per cent)' (Stockholm International Peace Research Institute, 2011). As far as export is concerned, '[t]he USA remains the world's largest exporter of military equipment, accounting for 30 per cent of global arms exports in 2006–10. During this period, 44 per cent of US deliveries went to Asia and Oceania, 28 per cent to the Middle East and 19 per cent to Europe' (Stockholm International Peace Research Institute, 2011). The meaning of arms-ammunition is so profound for the ruling echelons of both countries that they time and again struggle to prove their loyalty towards the construction of image. The race for justification is on. The maximum procurement is not needed but has become an image of justification constructed and imposed by MIC. Besides, according to Nick Turse, MIC has created or transformed United States' society into militarised society (Turse, 2008). The consequences upon Indians and Pakistanis remain tangible than a mere conjectural one.

Fourthly, imperialism paves the way for further expansion of capitalism[5]. Global capital cannot bypass both the countries who account for almost one billion and forty crore people. Wherever possible, global capital seeks help from different forces. American imperialism has worked differently for Pakistan and India. In the case of the former, pre-capitalist formation remains an important source of its success and expansion. India has exhibited nurturing and expansion of capitalism from within. Indian capitalists have corroborated with capitalism significantly but they cannot be called comprador. But, in any case, imperialism remains unaccountable to people's opinion. Goran Therborn suggests that 'US imperialism produces a very special variant of empire, which may be called Occidental despotism...Since its foundation, US imperialism has... had a remarkable lack of attraction to the routine of rules and the responsible exercise of power' (Therborn, 2006: 35). In turn, 'US pressure and local elite identification with the USA generate foreign and domestic policies in many countries that run against popular values, expectations and demands. To square the circle, then, local political elites have to devise ways of circumventing public opinion and democratic participation, and to do away with fair democratic procedures' (Therborn, 2006: 36). In many ways, imperialist intervention in Pakistan has produced innumerable surrogated institutions. In case of India, penetration into bureaucracy and ready availability of bourgeoisie parties to collaborate with USA, while bypassing the Parliament and without much debate are self-evident.

The signification of India and Pakistan on four accounts has germinated two impacts. Firstly, the purpose of ruling classes has been reduced in tune with 'existence', 'strategic', 'military industry complex' and 'imperialism'. The practice and theory have been greatly reduced to these spheres which were imposed on them as per the need of capitalism and imperialism. Secondly, coalescence history is marginalised. Dictated policy papers, manipulated white papers and act of killing each other remorselessly are the first negations of coalescence history. Revenges lead to killing. When killings become the habit of the state apparatus, people become the only and easy preys. Marginalisation or death of coalescence history paves the way for assertion of autonomy, by ruling echelons in the name of a better future.

Autonomous Zone

With or without territorial partition, supposed autonomous zones are always created. The creation serves the purpose of vertical and horizontal division. Vertical division establishes the hierarchy of ruling echelons. Verticality of hierarchies sets the option before people of governing classes. The fixity is laid bare. Over the years, choice synonymises few. The obvious outcome of verticality is horizontal subjects who 'seem' to be struggling even if minimum space is granted. The option is maximum and limited for them in respect to struggle. The 'structure-agency' debate is important here. For number of agencies, if option of struggle and its aim is confined within the niche of structure, struggle is bound to dry up eventually. If the aim is beyond the structure, it necessarily enables agencies to envisage and replace the structure.

In the context of India and Pakistan, an autonomous

structure is being created under the guardianship of the ruling echelons. In India, bureaucracy–industry–landlords with help from 'brahmanism' form the superstructure.

Envisaging and implementation of the Constitution was a great achievement for billions who are suppressed, class–caste wise. Proletariat and ascriptively subjugated groups that were denied even recognition, thought of taking some help from it. However, initial omission of compulsory distribution and laws against ascriptive birth, eventually catapulted these three groups in an unchallengeable position. It was even in their interest to turn the Constitution as a static document and for all distributional and caste-related practices, make it a reference point. There were two types of autonomous zones envisaged, created and implemented. First autonomous zone was directed against Pakistan. Any resemblance was severed. Greater role of India was perceived but equal role with Pakistan was *ipso facto* rejected. Second zone was internally imposed. Governing classes and governed classes were accepted and have been in full swing in three forms i.e. dynasty politics, billionaires' club and Hindutva. Others are also there that imbibe one of these as fringe actors. This scenario has produced great difficulty for the left and other formations to even contest. The empirical truth of election reveals that in many constituencies, the left cannot afford to fill the candidates due to the bullying impact of accumulation on the part of the trio.

The formation of Pakistan and the later development are two different issues. It would be erroneous to club them both together for the hermetic understanding of Pakistan's biography. Herein, Hamza Alavi becomes decisively significant. According to Alavi, '[n]o one has as yet examined the social forces that were actually responsible for the creation of Pakistan. Our true past has been snatched from us and lies buried where it cannot be found' (Alavi, 2002: 5120). Alavi explains that '[f]undamentalist Islamic ideology played no part in the origins of Pakistan, although contemporary ideologues of Islamic fundamentalism including academics, claim that it was Islamic ideology and slogans that created Pakistan and that they therefore have the right to decide its future' (Alavi, 2002: 5124). 'Modern Indian Muslim politics, in its origin, was ...quota politics and not a religious movement' (Alavi, 2002: 5121). 'The salariat [Ashraf] and the professionals had their own specific interests to pursue. Competition between these petit bourgeois Muslim and Hindu groups, shaped the policies of the All India Muslim League, and the Indian National Congress, respectively. They used concepts of Indian nationalism and Muslim nationalism, to legitimise their narrow class demands' (Alavi, 2002: 5120). Over the years, Muslim feudal grew in strength and succeeded to get a 'desired Pakistan'. Desired Pakistan denotes as sought by the feudal. Herein lays the nature, aspiration and struggle of commoners like peasants who were eventually cheated. 'The peasants were also promised abolition of zamindari. The Bengal peasantry was led to believe that Pakistan was going to be ruled by the peasants. If an ideology there was, it was a peasant ideology' (Alavi, 2002: 5124). 'But, in the end, the peasants were cheated, as they always are' (Alavi, 2002: 5124). Even after Independence, the Constitution promulgation and declaration of Pakistan as an Islamic republic took place in 1956 and 1991 witnessed the incorporation of Islamic Shariah Law into Legal Code.

If the creation of Pakistan was because of class interest then what could be the explanation of Islamisation of state apparatus despite M.A. Jinnah's famous statement:

> You may belong to any religion or caste or creed. That has nothing to do with the business of the state... We are starting with this fundamental principle that we are all citizens and equal citizens of the state...We should keep that in front of us as our ideal and you will find that in the course of time Hindus will cease to be Hindus and Muslims will cease to be Muslims, not in the religious sense because that is the personal faith of

each individual, but in the political sense, as citizens of the state (Jinna cited in Alavi, 2002: 5119).

What had happened to this promise? Alavi argues '[i]t was not until 1952 that Jinnah's unworthy successors turned away from that secular ideal and began to exploit the worn out rhetoric of religion to restore their failing political fortunes. They cried out that "Islam was in danger"! Coming from them, that was an insincere, bogus and empty slogan, when they had nothing positive to offer to the people' (Alavi, 2002: 5119). 'Slogans of "Islamic" ideology and "Islamic" identity were taken up to counter Bengali anger. Instead of looking at the underlying causes of Bengali discontent, they put forward an argument that we are all 'Muslims and Pakistanis' and therefore we cannot be Bengalis or Sindhis or Baluch or Pathan. This was an ethnic redefinition which had little to do with religious values as such. It was merely a bankrupt political argument which led only to disaster' (Alavi, 2002: 5119). The expansion of Islamicist is also linked with various external interventions. 'The Islamicist parties in Pakistan', writes Aijaz Ahmad, 'have far older origins but the Afghan jihad, conducted from Pakistani soil, catapulted them from their marginal positions in Pakistani society to the very centre, with immense material and organizational resources at their disposal; they played the key role in the ideological formation of what later became the Taliban' (Ahmad, 2008: 4).

Internal contradictions and external interventions were apt opportunities for the creation of autonomous zones. Religious fundamentalism has created vertical autonomy over billons of poor and the proletariat again. It is no wonder that certain families rule the country and similar families are largely feudal. The ruling class entails the governing political institutions along with military's top-notch positions. Autonomy *vis-à-vis* India is another aspect. The implication is meddling through farcical justification of ill-gotten thesis of 'clash of civilizations'. In a nutshell, autonomy has kept the poor, miserably away from justice and freedom, while a mirage of annihilation of each other is dramatised on every occasion. After 'successful' establishment of autonomy, India and Pakistan go for the contested zone.

Contested Zone

Contestation is an oft-repeated act of the ruling classes. The investment in contestation is gigantic. The core of contested zone is identified and deliberately made/becomes the on-going pandemonium of everyday life of two nations as if vitality and cruciality of other aspects are resolved or resolving is of no consequence. There are three contested zones which have been identified and gyrated through medium of every possible communication.

First contested zone is territorial zone and therein discontent. Jammu and Kashmir and Baluchistan may be a point of reference. Problems of each region are being highlighted. They are circulated and disseminated across the board. Now problems are omniscient. The people's discontent, development, religious and ethnic sovereignty, alienations and violence are attached with aforesaid regions. The problem is not that they are not true but who owns up to the problems. Naturally, each nation will disown the factors which led to such developments. The practice of shifting ownership becomes important. This is rigorously done in the form of lobbying, formations of a broad caucus, committed groups and so on. Mainstream media is a natural saviour of this important wont. What is unheard of and unclaimed is, as if both nations are progenitor of these developments that dismay people. They produce disenchantment, circulate as devastations and offer solutions as enchantment in the form of militarised society. So we have a travesty of enchantment for detachment. Detachment, as said and propagated, is the outcome of 'others' and enchantment is the attack. The trajectory of last six decades of both countries evinces the manoeuvre of shifting responsibility on the other and tragedy is that each is a germinator.

Second contested zone is the 'partition psyche'. The 'partition of territory' is construed as the partition psyche. In other words, in both countries' relations, there is a journey from partition of territory to partition psyche. Partition of territory was a historical juncture. Partition psyche is everyday lived and revered practice. Here, coalescence history is badly hurt. In place of construing India–Pakistan division as territorial division, the propagation harks back on the formulae of division of people. The commonality and the notion that we have been shaped, imbibed and metamorphosed by each other are squeezed out. Territorial division might prove to be an ephemeral distanciation, but partition psyche is an attempt towards permanent rupture. Permanent rupture is rejoiced and 'acted' by institutions.

The USA is the third contested zone. This is different from the USA's incessant intervention to shape the destiny of both India and Pakistan. Conversely, there is an institutional race for closer relationship with the USA. Institutional race works through three ways. Firstly, liberated virtues i.e. free capital and libertarian individualism are highlighted and celebrated. Secondly, they are presented as the only alternatives. Thirdly, institutional design is envisaged and implemented wherever possible. The implementation of new economic policies in 1991 in both countries was not coincidental. And both countries also desired to become closer to the USA. Generally and theoretically, capitalism remains unflourished without libertarian individualism. Nevertheless, in conflicts between these two in South Asia, capital is prioritised ironically as a result of initiation of political economy, where capital exists with the pre-capitalist virtues. Various military deals of Pakistan and the recent nuclear deal in India with the USA are justificatory illustration of the third contested zone.

Mutual Zone

Three contested zones give birth to the idea of contested engagement. It is propounded as a mutual zone. Overtly, contentious zones are avoided but streamlined as tension-reducing mechanisms. The idea is not the restoration of coalescence history but the evolution of the perspective which is contemporaneity. The possible benefits that accrue from the construction of history in the form of history of events is the desired interpretation and location of the past for the benefits of ruling echelons.

Two such areas have been 'in' in the discourse of mutual zone. The first is 'people-to-people-contact'. One remains baffled on the method of contact. The two media groups (The Jang Group in Pakistan and The Times of India in India) commence the process of 'aman ki asha' (hope for peace). Four means have been laid down: 'An honest and exhaustive debate on all contentious issues between the two countries, such as Kashmir, water, terrorism, Siachin, Sir Creek etc; Actively encourage and facilitate people-to-people contacts across the broadest possible spectrum; Initiate seminars, official and unofficial contacts, dialogues and meetings between Indians and Pakistanis, with a view to creating an enabling environment for both governments to dialogue on all outstanding issues; As the largest media groups in India and Pakistan, the Times of India Group and the Jang Group respectively, commit to using their print and electronic media to aggressively promote the benefits of peace in terms of economic development, uniting families, tourism, developing trade, and removing the obstacles to peace. We invite all other media to support this initiative in any and every way they can' (Aman Ki Asha, 2011). Ironically, these two media groups are infamous for their hawkish editorials and unrelenting, unrepentant support for neo-liberalism and military expansion. Besides, 'existence', 'strategic', 'military-industry-complex' and 'American imperialism' are squarely not touched. Though territorial zone is addressed, partition psyche is omitted. The role of USA is nowhere for repudiation. Without these, people-to-people contact remains repeated, farcical and a cyclical manoeuvre. These two types of state (India–Pakistan and United States) sponsored programmes are intended to mitigate violence against capital but not for restoration of coalescence history

The second arena is chalked out as the trade realm because 'trade is foreign policy'[6] (Kaufman, 2010: 2). Trade is considered beneficiary for both countries if it is done amicably and directly. It will be good and great after formation of regional trade bloc. At the outset, it seems a tangible idea and practice. But trade is sheer expression of contemporaneity. Relations are understood to be adjustable and need specific. Once the need is over, relations are of no use. Market relationship by way of trade is nothing more than reinforcing the logic of supra-structural adjustment when underneath rupture is allowed. The problem is that 'rupture' is always exploited. Trade can benefit and can also possibly become the common beneficiary but it certainly does not have potential to bridge the rupture.

By Way of Conclusions

Conclusions would not be sufficient here. In fact the offshoots of global signification and autonomous-contested-mutual zones of India-Pakistan relationship are external and internal consequences. On the external front, both countries are fighting to prove the global signification. The vantage point, process and end are guided by global signification which is the overt need of global capitalism. The second outcome is on internal front. The conflict between India and Pakistan, as discussed in previous pages, has strengthened two tendencies in each country. In fact, it is a result of all zones especially of the autonomous zone. The attempt to create autonomy (internal and external) has strengthened feudal forces and fundamentalism in Pakistan. Ruling classes, led by feudal forces, in the absence of massive capitalist formation, have protracted the class interest while maintaining autonomy from change and challenge. Fundamentalists have a swaying impact due to state policies and adoption and codifying Islamic remnants in the Constitution. Of course, as Alavi has pointed out, ruling echelons have nothing to offer than this.

As far as India is concerned, 'autonomy zone' has had two impacts. Initiation of mixed economy led to creation of state capitalism which in turn paved the way for capitalist growth.' 1980 onwards, India has witnessed opening up of market and massive sign of accumulation. Since then, spurious growth has taken place whereby billionaires' number has increased along with pauperisation of people. Capitalism/billionaires led India has maintained autonomy from pauperised people but is eagerly waiting to mix with the 'capitalist world'. Extractions from people and relaxation in taxes have strengthened their accumulative ability but expansion can take place only by way of integration in the capitalist world. Therefore, their natural envy with 'feudal' Pakistan leads to minimising its significance and influencing policies internally and globally to obstruct its development. Capitalism hardly has any take in feudalism for expansion purpose.

The utter dislike of Indian capitalism towards Pakistan gets the company of brahmanism which is the backbone of Hindutva and responsible for caste subjugation for two-third of Indian population. Hindutva's first and last enemy is Muslim minority in India and choice is between subjugation and annihilation. And they attempt to galvanise the anger of Indian people while linking Indian Muslims with Pakistan. Violence, hatred and humiliation of Indian Muslims have transformed and synonymised towards Pakistan. In the lexicon of Hindutva, Indian Muslim and Pakistan are synonymous. This serves two purposes. Firstly, it helps them to galvanise their position while keeping Muslim as the detracting group. As a result, their development becomes an anti-Majority issue which is a colossally farcical formulation. Constructed anger against Pakistan helps them elide internal contradiction like caste, class and gender discrimination while creating neo-brahmanism. Neo brahmanism does not question caste but celebrates caste, supporting Hindutva partially or fully.

Here, the role of transformative agency i.e. people also becomes crucial and critical. Moreover, this pessimistic elaboration of India–Pakistan relationship does not discount the role of agencies. Simply, structures can be fought and destroyed as they had been in the past. Role of progressive sections are very significant. First of all, coalescence history has to be restored in a sense that we all are affected by a single historical development in the sub-continent whose beneficiaries are feudalism, capitalism, fundamentalism and brahmanism/neo-brahmanism. Have-nots and the ascriptively subjugated ones have to be united for better relationship in place of fraught relationships which serve the cause of ruling echelons. This will be repudiation for those who understand the history from contemporaneity perspective while negating the commons.

NOTES

1. Actors' action or state behaviour vis-à-vis external atmosphere has been intrinsic theorisation of Kenneth Waltz (in the context of war) (Waltz, 1959), James Rosenau (theories and pre-theories of foreign policy) (Rosenau, 1966), Graham Allison (Rational Actor Model/state's acumen action in a tough international condition) (Allisson, 1969 & 1999).
2. I have discussed the entire issue partly in an earlier article; for details, please see (Rai, 2012a).
3. Sumit Sarkar highlights it in a different context. During National Democratic Alliance Regime, previously commissioned volumes on History were stalled because it did not suit the Hindutva propagators. He states that '[w]hat the RSS probably is afraid of is not the presence but an absence, the absence of Hindutva formations from any and

every confrontation with British rule, above all during the Quit India movement as well as the post-War upsurge during the winter of 1945-6 in major Indian cities that culminated in the Royal Indian Navy Mutiny of February 1946. Absence also from the rich history of debates and discussions about the content and meanings of freedom, apart from the narrowly communal' (Sarkar, 2005: 256).

4. However Praful Bidwai and Achin Vanaik present a different case. According to them,

   South Asia is not an area that requires urgent strategic attention from the US. It suffices if the US has a clear idea of what it wants strategically from the region. And what it does not want is to accept some unequivocal regional hegemon when it does not have so, and when India has still not shown the capacity to actually become such a hegemon. So why on earth should the US sacrifice or weaken its relationship to Pakistan just to please India? Even more ludicrous, why should the US give up its multiple options vis-à-vis China (and towards India) just to embrace the idea that a nuclear India would be an important ally in future US efforts to isolate the supposedly rising power of a twenty-first-century China? Some right-wing Republicans or Democrats in the US may join in with some Indian strategists to engage in such speculation, but that is all it is-speculation about possible future benefits. Such birds in the bush cannot be allowed to override in importance (let alone overturn) the management of the birds-in-the-hand reality of the existing complex pattern of US-China relations (Bidwai and Vanaik, 2000: 205).

5. Rosa Luxemburg makes an important observation in this regard. According to her,

   Thus capitalist accumulation as a whole, as an actual historical process, has two different aspects. One concerns the commodity market and the place where surplus value is produced – the factory, the mine, the agricultural estate. Regarded in this light, accumulation is a purely economic process, with its most important phase a transaction between the capitalist and wage labourer. In both its phases, however, it is confined to the exchange of equivalents and remains within the limits of commodity exchange. Here, in form at any rate, peace, property and equality prevail, and the keen dialectics of scientific analysis were required to reveal how the right of ownership changes in the course of accumulation into appropriation of other people's property, how commodity exchange turns into exploitation and equality becomes class-rule.

The other aspect of the accumulation of capital concerns the relations between capitalism and the non-capitalist modes of production which start making their appearance on the international stage. Its predominant methods are colonial policy, an international loan system—a policy of spheres of interest—and war. Force, fraud, oppression, looting are openly displayed without any attempt at concealment, and it requires an effort to discover within this tangle of political violence and contests of power the stern laws of the economic process.

Bourgeois liberal theory takes into account only the former aspect: the realm of 'peaceful competition', the marvels of technology and pure commodity exchange; it separates it strictly from the other aspect: the realm of capital's blustering violence which is regarded as more or less incidental to foreign policy and quite independent of the economic sphere of capital (Luxemburg, 1951: 452-453).

6. Joyce P. Kaufman makes an interesting observation. He states that

Most Americans pay little attention to foreign policy unless it appears to affect them directly. But foreign policy does affect everyone, not only because of threats of terrorist attacks or the danger of war, but for far more mundane reasons. Look at the label on the last article of clothing that you bought. Where was it manufactured ? In China? Bangladesh? What about your computer-Where was it made? When you called the technology help line because you have a problem with a product, where was that person sitting? Was it in the United States or in India? All of this is possible because of trade, and trade is foreign policy (Kaufman, 2010: 2).

References

Ahmad, A. (2000). *Lineages of the present: Ideology and politics in contemporary South Asia*. London: Verso.

Ahmad, A. (2008). Islam, Islamisms and the West. *Socialist Register, 44*, 1-37.

Alavi, H. (2002). Social forces and ideology in the making of Pakistan. *Economic and Political Weekly, 37*(51), 5119-5124.

All India Kisan Sabha (2010, January 7-10). Commission chapter on seed monopolies, genetically modified crops and Bt Brinjal, 32nd All India Conference, Guntur.

Allison, G. (1969). Conceptual models and the Cuban missile crisis. *American Political Science Review 63*(3), 689–718.

Allison, G. (1999). *The essence of decision: Explaining the Cuban missile crisis*. Boston: Little, Brown.

Aman Ki Asha (2011). Retrieved from http://amankiasha.com/faqs.asp

Ambedkar, B.R. (1979). Annihilation of caste. In V. Moon (Ed.), *Dr. Babasaheb Ambedkar, writings and speeches,* volume 1 (pp. 25-96). Bombay: Department of Education Publication, Government of Maharashtra.

Ambedkar, B.R. (1979). States and minorities: What are their rights and how to secure them in the constitution of free India. In V. Moon (Ed.), *Dr. Babasaheb Ambedkar, writings and speeches,* volume 1 (pp. 381-404). Bombay: Department of Education Publication, Government of Maharashtra.

Ambedkar, B.R. (1986). The future of parliamentary democracy. In B.R. Joshi, *Untouchable!: Voices of the dalit liberation movement* (pp. 39-40). New York: Zed Books.

Ambedkar, B.R. (1987). India and the pre-requisites of communism. In V. Moon (Ed.), *Dr. Babasaheb Ambedkar, writings and speeches,* volume 3 (pp. 93-228). Bombay: Department of Education Publication, Government of Maharashtra.

Ambedkar, B.R. (1990a). Pakistan or partition of India. In V. Moon (Ed.), *Dr. Babasaheb Ambedkar, writings and speeches,* volume 8 (pp. 369-480). Bombay: Department of Education Publication, Government of Maharashtra.

Ambedkar, B.R. (1990b). Mr. Gandhi and the emancipation of the untouchables. In V. Moon (Ed.), *Dr. Babasaheb Ambedkar, writings and speeches,* volume 9 (pp. 397-433). Bombay: Department of Education Publication, Government of Maharashtra.

Ambedkar, B.R. (1990c). Commercial relations of India in the middle ages or the rise of Islam and the expansion of Western Europe. In V. Moon (Ed.), *Dr. Babasaheb Ambedkar, writings and speeches,* volume 12 (pp. 1-30). Bombay: Department of Education Publication, Government of Maharashtra.

Ambedkar, B.R. (1991). Labour and parliamentary democracy. In V. Moon (Ed.), *Dr. Babasaheb Ambedkar, writings and speeches,* volume 10 (pp. 106-111). Bombay: Department of Education Publication, Government of Maharashtra.

Ambedkar, B.R. (2002). Caste, class and democracy. In V. Rodrigues (Ed.), *The essential writings of B.R. Ambedkar* (pp. 132-148). New Delhi: Oxford University Press.

Ambedkar, B.R. (2006). *The Buddha and his dhamma.* Delhi: Siddharth Books.

Ambedkar, B.R. (2009). *Mr. Gandhi and emancipation of the Untouchables.* Delhi: Siddharth Books.

Appadurai, A. (1996). *Modernity at large: Cultural dimensions of globalization.* Minneapolis: University of Minnesota Press.

Appignanesi, L. & Maitland, S. (Eds.) (1990). *The Rushdie file: Contemporary issues in the Middle East.* New York: Syracuse University Press.

Aristotle (1991). Politics book viii. In J. Barnes (Ed.), *The complete works of Aristotle,* volume 2 (pp. 1-175). Princeton, NJ: Princeton University Press.

Austin, G. (2008). *Working a democratic constitution: A history of the Indian experience.* New Delhi: Oxford University Press.

Bagchi, A.K. (1999). Globalisation, liberalisation and vulnerability:

India and third world. *Economic and Political Weekly, 34*(45), 3219-3230.

Barber, B. (2001). Challenges to democracy in an age of globalization. In R. Axtmann (Ed.), *Balancing democracy* (pp. 295-311). New York: Continuum.

Barnes, J. (Ed.) (1991a). *The complete works of Aristotle,* volume 1. Princeton, NJ: Princeton University Press.

Barnes, J. (Ed.) (1991b). *The complete works of Aristotle,* volume 2. Princeton, NJ: Princeton University Press.

Bhagwati, J. (2004). *In defence of globalization.* New Delhi: Oxford University Press.

Bidwai, P. &Vanaik, A. (2010). *New nukes: India, Pakistan and global nuclear disarmament.* New York: Interlink Books.

Bloom, A. (Ed.) (1979). *Emile or on education.* New York: Basic Books.

Boettke, P.J. (2006). Hayek and market socialism. In E.F. (Ed.), *The Cambridge companion to Hayek* (pp. 51-66). Cambridge: Cambridge University Press.

Bose, S. & Jalal, A. (2004). *Modern South Asia: History, culture and political economy.* London: Routledge.

Bukharin, N.I. & Preobrazhensky, E.A. (1969). *The abc of communism.* Baltimore: Penguin Books.

Burnet, J. (1980). *Aristotle on education: Extracts from the ethics and politics.* Cambridge: The Press Syndicate of the University of Cambridge.

Carr, E.H. (1987). *What is history?* New York: Penguin Books.

Chatterjee, P. (2004). *The politics of the governed: Reflections on popular politics in most of the world.* New York: Columbia University Press.

Chatterjee, P. (2011). *Lineages of political society: Studies in postcolonial democracy.* Ranikhet: Permanent Black.

Chibber, P. (2011). Dynastic parties: Organization, finance and impact. *Party Politics.*

Chomsky, N. (2004, September-October).War crimes and imperial fantasies. *International Socialist Review, 37.* Retrieved from http://www.isreview.org/issues/37/chomsy.shtml.

Cohen, S.P. (2004). *The idea of Pakistan.* Washington, D.C.: The Brookings Institution.

Collingwood, R.G. (1994). *The idea of history.* New York: Oxford University Press.

Croce, B. (1921). *Theory and history of historiography*. London: George G. Harrap and Co. Ltd.

Curren, R. (2007). *Philosophy of education: An anthology*. Oxford: Blackwell Publishing.

Dasgupta, B. (2005). *Globalisation: India's adjustment experience*. New Delhi: Sage Publications.

Eze, E.C. (2001). *Race and the enlightenment: A reader*. Oxford: Blackwell Publishers.

Fieldhouse, D.K. (1999). *The west and the third world: Trade, colonialism, dependence and development*. Oxford: Blackwell Publishers Ltd.

French, P. (2011). *An intimate biography of 1.2.billion people: India a portrait*. New Delhi: Allen Lane/Penguin Books.

Friedman, T. (2000). *Understanding globalization: The lexus and the olive tree*. New York: Anchor Books.

Gramsci, A. (2000). Ethical or cultural state. In D. Forgacs (Ed.), *The Gramsci reader: Selected writings 1916-1935* (p. 234). New York: New York University Press.

Gramsci, A. (2007). On education. In Q. Hoare and G.N. Smith (Eds.), *Selections from the prison notebooks of Antonio Gramsci* (pp. 24-43). Hyderabad: Orient Longman.

Guru, G. (2000). The man who thought differently: An inquiry into the political thinking of Dr. Ambedkar. In K.C. Yadav (Ed.), *From periphery to centre stage: Ambedkar, Ambedkarism and dalit future* (pp. 89-100). New Delhi: Manohar.

Guru, G. (2002). Ambedkar's idea of social justice. In G. Shah (ed.), *Dalit identity and politics* (pp. 160-194). New Delhi: Sage Publications.

Guru, G. (Ed.) (2009). *Humiliations: Claims and context*. New Delhi: Oxford University Press.

Habib, I. (2000). *Essays in Indian history: Towards a Marxist perspective*. New Delhi: Tulika.

Harvey, D. (2003). *The new imperialism*. New York: Oxford University Press.

Held, D. & McGrew, A. (2000). The great globalization debate: An introduction. In D. Held & A. McGrew (Eds.), *The global transformations reader: An introduction to the globalization debate*. Cambridge: Polity Press.

Held, D. (2005). Globalization: The dangers and the answers. In A. Barnett, D. Held & C. Henderson (Eds.), *Debating globalization* (pp. 1-36). Cambridge: Polity Press.

Hollander, J.H. (1911). The development of the theory of money from Adam Smith to David Ricardo. *The Quarterly Journal of Economics, 25* (3), 429-470.

Hull, D.L. (1997). What's wrong with invisible-hand explanations? *Philosophy of Science, 64* (supplement), 117-S126.

Huntington, S. (1996). *The clash of civilizations and the remaking of world order*. New York: Simon and Schuster.

Kant, I. (1994). Transition from popular moral philosophy to a metaphysics of morals. In I. Kant, *Ethical philosophy: Grounding for the metaphysics of morals, metaphysical principles of Virtue* (pp.19-48). Indianapolis: Hackett Publishing Company.

Kapur, D., Prasad, C.B., Pritchett, L. & Babu, D.S. (2010). Rethinking inequality: Dalits in Uttar Pradesh in the market reform era. *Economic and Political Weekly*, xlv(35), 39-49.

Kaufman, J.P. (2010). *A concise history of U.S. foreign policy*. Lanham, Maryland: Rowman & Littlefield Publishing Group, Inc.

Kaviraj, S. (1986). Indira Gandhi and Indian politics. *Economic and Political Weekly, 21*(38/39), 1697-1708.

Keer, D. (2009). *Dr. Ambedkar: Life and mission*. Mumbai: Popular Prakashan.

Kosambi, D.D. (1996). *An introduction to the study of Indian history*. Mumbai: Popular Prakashan.

Kothari, R. (1964). The congress system in India. *Asian Survey, 4*(12), 1161-1173.

Kuber, W.N. (2001). *Dr Ambedkar: A critical study*. New Delhi: Peoples' Publishing House.

Lenin, V.I. (1978). *Speech at the first all-Russia congress on education*. In *Collected works*, volume 28 (pp. 85-88). Moscow: Progress Publishers.

Locke, J. (1996). Mathematics. In R.W. Grant and N. Tarcow (Eds.), *Some thoughts concerning education & Of the conduct of the understanding* (pp. 179-181). Indianapolis: Hackett Publishing Company.

Lodge, R.C. & Frank, S. (2000). *Plato's theory of education*. London: Routledge.

Luxemburg, R. (1951). *The accumulation of capital*. New Haven: Yale University Press.

Mander, H. (2002). Status of dalits and agenda for state intervention. In G. Shah (Ed.), *Dalits and state* (pp. 147-170). New Delhi: Concept Publishing House.

Marx, K. & Engels, F. (1976). German ideology. In *Karl Marx and Frederick Engels collected works*, volume 5, *1845-1847* (pp. 19-539). New York: Progress Publishers.

Marx, K. & Engels, F. (1999). The manifesto of communist party. In P. Karat (Ed.), *A world to win: Essays on the communist manifesto* (pp. 87-130). New Delhi: LeftWord.

Menon, N. & Nigam, A. (2007). *Power and contestation: India since 1989*. New York: Zed Books.

Mill, J.S. (2003). *On liberty*. London: Yale University Press.

Nigam, A. (2002a). In Search of a bourgeoisie: Dalit politics enters a new phase. *Economic and Political Weekly, 37* (13), 1190-1193.

Nigam, A. (2002b). Rashtravadi chintan se pare, vishwayan aur dalit rajniti. In A.K. Dubey (Ed.), *Adhunikta ke aiene mein dalit* (pp. 397-403). New Delhi: Vani Prakashan and CSDS.

Omvedt, G. (2005). Capitalism and globalisation, dalits and adivasis. *Economic and Political Weekly, xl* (47), 4881-4884.

Pai, S. (2010). *Development State and the Dalit Question in Madhya Pradesh: Congress response*. New Delhi: Routledge.

Parekh, B. (Ed.)(1990). *Free speech*. London: Commission for Racial Equality.

Parekh, B. (2000). *Rethinking multiculturalism: Cultural diversity and political theory*. London: Macmillan.

Patnaik, P. (2003). *The retreat to unfreedom: Essays on the emerging world order*. New Delhi: Tulika Publishers.

Patnaik, P. (2005). *The economics of the new phase of imperialism*. Retrieved from http://www.macroscan.org/anl/aug05/pdf/Economics_New_Phase.pdf.

Pavelec, S.M. (2010). *The military-industrial complex and American society*. Santa Barbara : ABC-CLIO, LLC.

Plato (1970). *Plato: The laws*. London: Penguin Classics.

Plato (2003). *The republic*. Cambridge: Cambridge University Press.

Prasad, C.B. (2004). *Dalit diary: 1999-2003, reflections on apartheid in India*. Chennai: Navayana Publishing.

Prasad, C.B. (2009a, April 26). Globalization and the caste order. Retrieved from http://www.chandrabhanprasad.com/frmGlobalization.aspx (Accessed on April 26, 2009).

Prasad, C.B. (2009b). Change in Capitalism. *The Pioneer*, January 11.

Prashad, V. (2005, September-October). The Caste struggle: Review of dalit dairy by Chandrabhan Prasad and Buffalo nationalism by Kancha Ilaiah. *Biblio*.

Rai, D. (2012a). India and Pakistan: Exploring the tangibility of three zones. *Think India Quarterly,* 14(4), 90-102.

Rai, D. (2012b). Rescinding freedom via Ambedkar. *Pragoti.* Retrieved from http://www.pragoti.in/node/4684.

Rosenau, J. (1971). Pre-theories and theories of foreign policy (1966). In James Rosenau (Ed.), *In the scientific study of foreign policy* (pp. 95–151). New York: Free Press.

Rothschild, E. (1992). Adam Smith and conservative economics. *The Economic History Review,* 45(1), 74-96.

Rothschild, E. (1994). Adam Smith and the invisible hand. *The American Economic Review,* 84(2), 319-322.

Rousseau, J.J. (1979). Book i. In Jean Jacques Rousseau, *Emile or On education* (37-76). New York: Basic Books.

Rushdie, S. (1990). An open letter to the Indian Prime Minister. In L. Appignanesi & S. Maitland (Eds.), *The Rushdie file: Contemporary issues in the Middle East* (pp. 34-36). New York: Syracuse University Press.

Russell, B. (1996). Freedom and government. In John G. Slater & Peter Kollner (Eds.), *A fresh look at empiricism: 1927-42 (Collected papers of Bertrand Russell,* volume 10*)* (pp. 436-449). London: Routledge.

Said, E.W., Ali, A.S., Abu-Lughod, I., Bilgrami, A. & Ahmad, E. (1989). The satanic verses. *The New York Review of Books.* Retrieved from http://www.nybooks.com/articles/archives/1989/mar/16/the-satanic-verses/?pagination=false.

Sarkar, S. (2005). *Beyond nationalist frames: Relocating postmodernism, Hindutva, history.* Delhi: Permanent Black.

Sengupta, S. (2008, August 29). Crusader sees wealth as cure for caste bias. *The New York Times.* Retrieved from http://www.nytimes.com/2008/08/30/world/asia/30caste.html?pagewanted=all&_r=0.

Shah, G. (2002). Dalits and the State: An overview. In G. Shah (Ed.), *Dalits and state* (pp. 15-39). New Delhi: Concept Publishing House.

Small, R. (2005). *Marx and education.* Hampshire: Ashgate Publishing.

Smith, A. (2003). *Wealth of nations.* New York: Bantam Book.

Smith, V.L. (1998). The two faces of Adam Smith. *Southern Economic Journal,* 65 (1), 2-19.

Stockholm International Peace Research Institute (2011, March 14). Retrieved from http://www.sipri.org/media/pressreleases/armstransfers

The Bhopal Declaration: Chartering a New Course for Dalits for the 21st Century (2002, January 12-13). Bhopal: Bhopal Conference.

Therborn, G. (2006). The pole and the triangle: US power and the triangle of the Americas, Asia and Europe. In V.R. Hadiz (Ed.), *Empire and neoliberalism in Asia* (pp. 23-37). London: Routledge.

Thorat, S. (2009). *Dalits in India: Search for a Common Destiny*. New Delhi: Sage Publications.

Tomaik, J.J. (1974). Fifty-five years of Soviet education: The grandeur of the vision and the might of reality-united, separated or forever divorced? In T.G. Cook (Ed.),*The history of education in Europe* (pp. 37-52). London: Methuen & Co Ltd.

Turse, N. (2008). *The complex: How the military invades our everyday Lives*. New York: Metropolitan Books.

Waltz, K.N. (1959). *Man, the state, and war: A theoretical analysis*. New York: Columbia University Press.

Waltz, K.N. (1979). *Theory of international politics*. London: Addison-Wesley Publishing Company.

Waterman, A.M.C. (2002). Economics as theology: Adam Smith's wealth of nations. *Southern Economic Journal*, 68(4), 907-921.

Wolff, J. (1991). *Robert Nozick: Property, justice and the minimal state*. Cambridge: Polity Press.

Zelliot, E. (1996). *From untouchable to dalit: Essays on Ambedkar Movement*. New Delhi: Manohar Publications.

Zelliot, E. (2001). The meaning of Ambedkar. In G. Shah (Ed.), *Dalit identity and politics* (pp. 129-142). New Delhi: Sage Publications.

Index